Published by: Knewasser Productions ®

Publisher: Jessica Knewasser

ISBN: 978-1-7334552-2-0
eISBN: 978-1-7334552-3-7

● kpmanga.com
● instagram.com/knewasser_productions/
● facebook.com/KnewasserProductions/
● tapas.io/knewasserproductions

101 Relatable Monologues, April 2025
Published by Knewasser Productions™
Bordentown, NJ 08505. © 2025 Jessica Knewasser.
All Rights Reserved. 101 Relatable Monologues
content, artwork, and characters
are created by Jessica Knewasser 2025. ©
The Knewasser Productions ® name and logo
are trademarks of Jessica Knewasser.
The events, institutions, and characters
presented in this book are all fictional.
Any resemblance to actual persons, living
or dead, is purely coincidental. No portion
of this publication may be reproduced, by any
means, without the express written permission
of the copyright holder.

Printed in USA

10 9 8 7 6 5 4 3 2 1

Table of Contents

Preface - 9

Dedication - 12

60-Second Monologues - 13

Number 1: Featured: Memories of the Sky - 14

Number 2: The Truth about your Singing - 16

Number 3: Man Found After Explosion - 17

Number 4: Clean Up Tasks - 19

Number 5: Featured from Over My Dead Body, Volume 1: Chapter 3 - 21

Number 6: Angry New Patient - 23

Number 7: My Apartment is Haunted - 25

Number 8: I'm Not Cutting the Grass, No -27

Number 9: Lobster Salad - 28

Number 10: Pepper as a Present - 29

Number 11: Scheduling Appointment for Spouse - 30

Number 12: Featured from Over My Dead Body, Volume 1: Chapter 1 -31

Number 13: Noisy Upstairs Neighbors Take a Shower - 32

Number 14: I'll Give You a Warning - 33

Number 15: Don't You Come in Here - 35

Number 16: When Your Boss Wants You to Put Out a Fire - 37

Number 17: That's Because It's Not... - 38

Number 18: New Jerseyans Don't Pump Gas - 40

Number 19: One Bag, Got It? - 42

Number 20: Featured from Over My Dead Body, Volume 2: Chapter 7 - 44

Number 21: You were Jealous? - 45

Number 22: News Anchor - 47

Number 23: The Other Mermaid - 49

Number 24: Six Month Anniversary - 51

Number 25: Let Me Reintroduce Myself - 52

Number 26: Featured from My First Manga: Ryuu Romance - 54

90-Second Monologues - 56

Number 27: Widow on her Wedding Day - 57

Number 28: Featured from Powerless the Opening of the Story - 59

Number 29: Traitor to the Republic - 61

Number 30: Good Dog Goes Bad - 63

Number 31: A Good Snap - 65

Number 32: No Teeth... - 67

Number 33: Let There be Rain - 69

Number 34: Extractions - 71

Number 35: Featured from Future Project: Dating AI - 73

Number 36: Get Out! - 75

Number 37: I Didn't Know - 77

Number 38: Why Can't I Just Say No? - 79

Number 39: Why Would You Watch This Garbage? - 81

Number 40: Why Is He Crying? - 83

Number 41: The Sandbox - 85

Number 42: Darby, I'm Furious - 87

Number 43: While the Whole World Slept - 89

Number 44: The Worst Pet - 91

Number 45: Cricket Flour Bread - 93

Number 46: Paint and Sip - 95

Number 47: The Thoughtful Spider - 97

Number 48: Gacies on a Stick - 99

Number 49: Free Entertainment - 101

Number 50: No Jury Duty For Me Please - 103

Number 51: I Can't Get Sick! - 105

Number 52: This is My Micromanager - 107

Number 53: Retail Story: Headset Radio - 109

Number 54: Toddler Talk - 111

Number 55: The Chilling Churner - 113

Number 56: Eyes and Ears Open - 115

Number 57: You Have a Cat, Right? - 117

Number 58: F*ck Friday - 119

Number 59: Overwhelmed - 121

Number 60: How Did This Happen? - 123

Number 61: Lasting Pain - 125

Number 62: A Complex Case - 127

Number 63: Do I Really Have to Date? - 129

Number 64: What Else Do You Want to Do? - 131

Number 65: A Case in the Night Owl's Favor - 133

Number 66: What People Say Is About Them, But Should I Hear About Me? - 135

Number 67: What Happened? - 137

Number 68: Elizabeth Tower and Big Ben - 139

Number 69: Why the Love Potion Didn't Work - 141

Number 70: Daisy Award - 143

Number 71: My Kitten's Rescue - 145

Number 72: I Just Love to Talk - 147

Number 73: Not a Good Husband - 149

Number 74: You Did Your Best - 151

Number 75: Vincent's Muse - 153

Number 76: The Persian Messenger - 155

Number 77: You Never Disappoint Me, Darling - 157

120-Second Monologues - 159

Number 78: My Feelings of Love are not Crazy - 160

Number 79: The Abandoned Gray - 162

Number 80: Truth or Dare - 164

Number 81: What Do You Want to Do? - 166

Number 82: Saving a Child from a Predator - 168

Number 83: What Are You Doing in the Bushes? - 170

Number 84: I Left - 172

Number 85: Roommate Interrogation - 174

Number 86: I Hold a Candle - 176

Number 87: The Last Time I Saw Him - 178

Number 88: Help Us from Our Godfather - 181

Number 89: Worst Shopping Experience - 183

Number 90: The Most Horrifying Place - 185

Number 91: I'll Show You How It's Done, Little Boy - 187

Number 92: A Best Friend - 189

Number 93: Why Do They Keep Him? - 191

Number 94: My First Roller Coaster Ride - 193

Number 95: Cookie - 195

Number 96: Featured from All Because of an Apple - 197

Number 97: She Owes Me - 199

Number 98: Pappy's Blanket - 201

Number 99: Happy Birthday to my Dear Uncle - 203

Number 100: A Man Dies on a Deserted Island - 205

Number 101: Doing This for Love - 207

About the Author - 209

Index - 211

In Loving Memory of Jerry Mamola - 215

Preface

This monologue book is a compilation of many stories I've written from as far back as my high school years to scenarios based on my current life experiences. My goal was to make a relatable piece that could be used by all actors whether in the amateur world or the professional one.

I tried very hard to make each monologue as gender neutral as possible so any actor could use them. I even went as far as to pick more gender neutral names whenever the character has a name for his or herself. Oftentimes, I may have chosen to pick a female pronoun to describe a character. That's because I didn't feel like writing his or her or his/hers or them or whatever combination. In traditional writing in those scenarios, the default is often the male pronoun, but I chose female since most of these stories are from my perspective. I wanted to make this clear so other people who do not use female pronouns don't need to feel like they cannot use that monologue. Feel free to use these in any audition that you choose!

As mentioned before, some of these monologues are purely fictional. Many come from stories I wrote in my teen years. I simply cannot believe what these little short stories turned into! For years I thought that they would never see the light of day, but through this book, I'm seeing them reborn in the absolute best way possible! I'm so proud of them and what they turned into! I've learned to never dismiss a work of art that I love as a waste of time. This book is proof that it's not!

Some of these stories are a lot less fictional. Unfortunately, I had some experiences that I've struggled to cope with. So in those cases, I found turning my experiences into monologues therapeutic, as if receiving justice for what

I've been through. "Hahaha, you were mean to me and now I'm gonna profit off this and you're not!" –Basically... Not all the fictional stories are from my teen years though! Writing has always been my passion and some of these stories actually are brand new specifically for this piece! I tried to create new stories in the gaps between my life experiences and current fictional stories by thinking of roles that an actor might need a monologue for. For example, I've never been to jail, [I hope I never do] but with popular shows involving the criminal justice system, I wanted to include something that could aid in an actor getting that kind of role. I have 101 of these included in here, so I hope there's something for every role!

I've also included a couple monologues that come from my manga series, Over My Dead Body. I'm publishing this book under my own company, Knewasser Productions, and I felt including a couple monologues from the piece that started my business tied all my passions into one! Those definitely have more character specifics, but as I said before, use them to get your next role! If you like these monologues included in here, please consider checking out the series!

Lastly, you may be wondering why I decided to make this 101 monologues and not stop at 100. 101 is actually an homage to 1001 Arabian Nights. At the time of writing this, I admittedly have a huge crush on a middle eastern man who loves stories. This makes me feel like Scheherazade in a way [Well, minus all the murder]. I hope he will one day read my work and become as big of a fan of me as I am of him. I never would have pursued acting if it wasn't for him. He showed me the possibilities of what a musical and acting career could actually look like by example. For some reason, he made me feel like it wasn't just a crazy pipe dream to pursue acting and singing. After the first time I ever saw him perform, I noticed that I could hit a high note that I've never been able to hit

10

before. My feelings for him, along with some very skilled coaching from one of my closest friends, has guided me through this project. While I thought writing 1001 monologues would be a little much for the time being, I felt like removing a zero still honored the homage I was going for.

I wish all my readers good luck on all of your creative goals! Keep performing! Keep trying! Keep getting inspired to do more!

Love,

Jessica Knewasser

Dedication

This book is dedicated to my close friend and Life Coach, Barbara Anne Gardenhire-Mills.
This piece could not be possible without her guidance through my transformative journey to become my optimal self.

I will always remember to repeat:

–What people say is about them. What I hear is about me.

–No one else is allowed to write my story.

Among other mantras.

Note to my reader: If therapy is no longer working for you, maybe you are perfectly functional and ready for the next step in your journey. Consider getting a life coach today!

I also wanted to dedicate this to my parents: Joseph and Laura Knewasser

Thank you for supporting my newest, among many artist goals! Thank you for being so supportive of *Over My Dead Body* and I know you will treat this book the same.

60-Second Monologues

Number 1: Featured: Memories of the Sky

Time Length: 60 seconds

Categories/ Theme: Dramatic, Fantasy, Adventure, Psychological, Misunderstanding

Scene: Amalia runs from the guards after she naively mentions being a Sky Pirate even though she's not and she's suffering from amnesia.

What have I gotten myself into? Who are these guards chasing me? What do they have against Sky Pirates? Is Tadahiro a bad guy? Am I some kind of accomplice? That can't be right; I was going to pay for the produce and stuff with money. So why are they calling me a thief? Are Sky Pirates really thieves? Is that what Tadahiro is? A criminal?

Whether he is or not is something I should worry about later. I may not actually be a Sky Pirate like him, but that "Old Papa" guy has already labeled me as one. If the guards catch me now, they won't believe my side of the story—especially when I'm just a girl with amnesia. I'm sure they've heard that excuse before.

What would they do to me if they caught me? I don't want to find out, so I have no choice but to find Tadahiro. He's the only one I can trust.

My heart is pounding, and it's getting harder and harder to breathe. I'm not sure how much longer I can keep running away from them.

I have to find Tadahiro! Where could he have gone?

Wait! Is that him? It is!

Tadahiro! Tadahiro! Help! I-can't-run-anymore...

Number 2: The Truth about your Singing

Time Length: 60 seconds

Categories/ Theme: Dramatic, Self-Discovery, Friendship, Slice of Life, Bullying

Scene: Two friends discuss a traumatic event from middle school.

Honestly, it was really weird. I remember when you first sang in front of the whole class. Everyone was raving about it. "Oh my gosh! Did you hear Alex sing? Wasn't that amazing? It was so good!"

And then, the very next day, everyone was saying they hated your voice and that it was bad... I don't get it.

I thought it was good! You always sounded amazing! I used to get so jealous, but then the whole class acted like you were terrible. They didn't even explain why they disliked it or why they changed their minds overnight. All they said was, "Alex sucks. Alex can't sing."

Even if you couldn't sing, I don't know what the big deal was! You still got up there and performed in front of everyone! Good or bad, that took a lot of courage. I couldn't do that... The fact that you did should earn you respect from everyone. They had no reason to treat you that way!

But I want you to know that they did initially like it because it was truly good! You have to believe that! Whatever made them change their minds had nothing to do with your talent. Keep singing because you're amazing!

Number 3: Man Found After Explosion

Time Length: 60 seconds

Categories/Theme: Dramatic, Suspense, Overcoming Adversity, Isolation, Adventure

Scene: There was an explosion on a deserted island. The only known occupant who was trapped there after an aviation accident is reacting to the scene.

The world finally stopped shaking. I can't believe something could shake the earth for this long. What even caused this? Is it safe to return to my shelter? Is it even still there?

Everything looks exactly the same—sand, palm trees, and oh good! The parachute is still draped on my shelter! It must still be intact! Thank goodness!

Did I imagine the explosion yesterday? Am I starting to go crazy after being alone for so long?
Wait. What is that? Is that... a person?

(Run over to the person)

Hey, Mister! Wake up!

No response. Is he dead? Ugh, just my luck... The first person I see in over a year and it's a corpse... Dammit!

(Kicks the body in the leg)

Oh, sorry... Didn't mean to disrespect the dead...

But there's still quite a bit of color in his face.

(Bend down to check for a pulse)

I don't believe it! There's an actual pulse! He's alive!

But why is he here? And why won't he wake up?

Hey! Hey, wake up!

(Pause, then with growing urgency)

Come on, please... Wake up!

(Softly) Please... I don't want to be alone anymore.

Number 4: Clean Up Tasks

Time Length: 60 seconds

Categories/ Theme: Dramatic, Workplace, Conflict, Misunderstanding, Authority

Scene: A manager is trying to get a team to clean up after an event. One member is new to the team and was missing. The manager berates the team member unfairly. When the team member explains the manager does not apologize.

Great job everyone! Now you saw on the bulletin board who is responsible for what.

Jane and Megan, you guys are on cleaning duty in the women's changing area.

Avery, you are in charge of the—where is Avery? Avery left? Avery wasn't supposed to leave. Okay, good to know.

Okay Tom, Lance, George, over here. Let's start taking this apart.

Oh? There's Avery. Avery, you are in charge of the men's changing area. It was on the bulletin board. We all have tasks to do. Go!

Okay, James, let's take this apart here. Hold this for me.

Ah! AVERY! YOU ARE SUPPOSED TO BE CLEANING THE MEN'S CHANGING ROOM! THAT INCLUDES SWEEPING, CLEANING THE SINKS, TAKING OUT THE TRASH,

CLEANING OFF THE TABLES, CLEANING OFF THE CHAIRS, AND— What?

You were asking all the guys if they took all personal items out of the room? That's not—That's what the director asked you to do? Fine...

(Turn away from Avery, noticing the uncomfortable looks from others)

James, hold this here. Max, do you have the mallet?

Number 5: Featured from Over My Dead Body, Volume 1: Chapter 3

Time Length: 60 seconds

Categories/ Theme: Humorous, Supernatural, Romance, Afterlife, Conflict, Frustration

Scene: Mayumi, a ghost girl, just attempted to kill Hiroki, a living college student in his bedroom. As a ghost she has some limitations as to what she can do as a ghost.

Good morning, Hiroki! Don't you think you would be more comfortable on the bed? There was no need to fall on the floor.

Don't call me, "Ghost Lady!" It's Mayumi. What am I doing here? I'm here to kill you of course!

Don't tell me you were gay this whole time! Liar! I saw the way you looked at that foreign girl! Your eyes got all googly-eyed and everything!

A girl like her won't last. Sure, you just wanted to try the fruit of a foreign land, but I'm certain you will forget all about her once she returns to America.

But we can spend eternity together. We wouldn't even need to part after death because we'd already be dead. Doesn't that sound fun?

Ugh! Fine! If you won't join me on your own, I'll just have to make you!

(Mayumi goes to grab a knife and attempts to point it at Hiroki, but if goes through her hands)

Haha! Ah! Oh no! It went right through my hand! Hahahaha... Technical difficulties...

(Mayumi turns to grab the knife again and she cannot lift it.)

I'll kill you in just a moment... Ugh. Come on stupid knife! Maybe if–No–What if–No! Okay, maybe the other hand–ugh... It's no use...

(Mayumi turns back to Hiroki who seems to be leaving)

Get back here! I'm not done killing you yet! We were meant to be together and you know it!

Number 6: Angry New Patient

Time Length: 60 seconds

Categories/Theme: Humorous, Workplace, Communication, Customer Service, Technology

Scene: A dental receptionist receives a phone call from an insecure patient with a terrible connection

Ugh! That ring! Who ever thought that sound was an acceptable noise for a phone call?!

(Answer the phone)

Thank you for calling Brooktoll Dental, how can I help you?

Hello? Brooktoll Dental, how can I help you?

Oh there we go. I can hear you now. Sorry, my phone is really old. How can I assist you today?

Okay, you would like to schedule an appointment? Are you a new patient? You said you were a new patient right?

Okay, great. Let me get your information. We can see new patients on Friday the 7th. Does that work for you?

Friday the 7th works for you? Yes? Okay great. What insurance do you have so I know you're in network? You said Horizons, right? Horizons? Okay great! We're in network!

What is the patient's name? Sorry—one more time. I'm sorry I still didn't get that. F as in Frank?

Oh! Oh... I'm so sorry... Look, my phone is from the 80's, so I really can't hear what your–

Oh... She hung up...

Oh...she said Samantha... I thought she said Fernanda...

Number 7: My Apartment is Haunted

Time Length: 60 second

Categories/ Theme: Humorous, Supernatural, Friendship, Misunderstanding, Slice of Life

Scene: A guest who has likely never been in an old apartment before hears a bunch of loud noises. The tenant doesn't like the noises either and jokes that it's haunted. The guest takes her word seriously and panics.

What was that noise? Wait! What? Haunted? You think this place is haunted? You're joking, right?

Well, yeah, I get that this is an old building, but surely there aren't any ghosts here. What? The lady upstairs died when you first moved in? S-so you think it's her? She's the one making all that noise? You felt her presence right after she died?

There's that noise again! Why does it sound like the ceiling is creaking? Are ghost footprints really that loud?

Why are you so calm? You live in a haunted house—well, apartment—but still! How can you stand it?

You just acknowledge it, and it makes it easier to accept... Well, I'm acknowledging that I don't like it here, and it gives me the creeps! Have fun with your spooky friend! I'm leaving!

No! I'm leaving! Where is my bag? Wait, what? Those are your new neighbors upstairs? They're alive, not some ghost? Marie! You scared me!

So you like to joke that your apartment is haunted because the noise bothers you... How is that better?

Ugh, just turn the movie back on!

(Pause)

Oh my gosh! They are noisy! I get what you mean...

Number 8: I'm Not Cutting the Grass, No

Time Length: 60 seconds

Categories/ Theme: Humorous, Relationships, Morality, Slice of Life, Conflict, Anxiety

Scene: A neighbor is about to cut the grass, but his neighbor comes outside to hang up her laundry. The neighbor quickly tells her that he was not going to cut the grass. He's a little afraid of her.

What time is it now? 11:30 AM. Hm... Not a bad time to cut the grass. Yeah, I think I'm gonna cut the grass.

Just gotta go uncover my tractor and, oh. My neighbor just came outside. It looks like she's coming this way. Maybe she's picking something up over here and going back inside? Nope, she's waving at me. She specifically wants to talk to me.

(Exhale)

Hello, Mrs. Jones! How are you doing today? Me? I'm good, thank you for asking. What? No, I wasn't gonna cut the grass. You want to hang your laundry up on the clothesline? Have at it! No, I really wasn't gonna cut the grass. Don't worry about it. I was just looking at my tractor because–it's broken! Yeah! I need to go get parts for it. That's why I was looking at it just now. Enjoy your day, Mrs. Jones!

(Walk away)

Phew... Glad I didn't get her upset...

Number 9: Lobster Salad

Time Length: 60 seconds

Categories/ Theme: Humorous, Communication, Conflict, Slice of Life, Customer Service, Food

Scene: A waiter gets the customer's order wrong, but the waiter insists that the customer ordered lobster salad.

Great! Our food is here! Oh, that looks so good, John. What did you order, Janine?

Um, excuse me. This isn't what I ordered. Yes, my name is El. El ordered the lobster salad? No, I ordered buffalo wings. Yeah, I'm pretty sure I ordered buffalo wings. Did someone else order the lobster salad? No one ordered it? Yes, I'm El, but I didn't order the lobster salad.

I told you, I ordered buffalo wings. Where did the lobster salad even come from? I don't see it on the menu. Where is it? Oh, it's a summer special? Well, I still want the buffalo wings. Yes, I'm sure. No, I don't want the lobster salad with the buffalo wings. Just the buffalo wings and a refill on the soda. Thank you!

Number 10: Pepper as a Present

Time Length: 60 seconds

Categories/ Theme: Humorous, Family, Relationships, Thematic, Slice of Life

Scene: A mother explains to her daughter why she gave her daughter's ex pepper for Christmas that one year.

Yes, your ex was so particular about everything. I felt like no matter what I did, he was judging me. Nothing I did seemed to sit right with him. He was so dismissive, as if my job as your mother was over and it was time for me to go. I hated that.

So on Christmas, I didn't want to exclude him—wouldn't have been very Christian of me—but after the way he treated me all year, I just didn't have it in me to go all out and buy him an amazing gift. Honestly, I don't think I could find him an amazing gift even if I tried my best and spent a ton of money. He would have found something wrong with it! So, I decided not to even try.

That's why I bought him pepper—just regular pepper from the grocery store. He had just moved into his new house, and you said he liked to grill. I didn't want to risk buying him a flavor he didn't like, so I went with pepper. How could he fault pepper? It goes on everything! (Laughs)

I think that's rather clever of me. I didn't like him because he didn't like me, but I still wanted to be nice since he was dating my daughter. So, I bought him pepper.

(Laughs) And see, you said he didn't complain! Even he couldn't fault pepper!

Number 11: Scheduling Appointment for Spouse

Time Length: 60 seconds

Categories/ Theme: Humorous, Relationships, Slice of Life, Health, Communication

Scene: Spouse makes an appointment over the phone for his wife.

Hello, this is Ari Weber calling. I called you people earlier today and was put on hold for 45 minutes. This is the second time calling you today and I got someone on the phone immediately. Could you explain why that happened? Uh huh.

Well, I'm calling on behalf of my wife. I need to make an appointment for a new patient. Her name is Ruby Weber. 5/25/54. Medicare. No, it needs to be after 12 PM. She has mobility issues and will need time to get transportation. Tomorrow at 1:30 PM? That should work. Thank you.

(Hangs up) (grumbles) (Calls wife)

Yes, hello Ruby. Yes, I made the appointment. Tomorrow at 1:30. Tomorrow. Tomorrow. You can't do tomorrow? Ruby, I'm not calling them again.

(Sighs heavily)

Ruby... Fine! I'll give you the number and you can change it yourself! Okay Bye!

(Sigh...)

Number 12: Featured from Over My Dead Body, Volume 1: Chapter 1

Time Length: 60 seconds

Categories/ Theme: Humorous, Supernatural, Romance, Afterlife, Frustration

Scene: Hiroki is telling Mayumi that he has no interest joining her in the afterlife. He is trying to be calm but she's testing his nerves.

Look Ghost Lady, I didn't wanna say this, but you had no business following me in the first place. It's your own fault that you weren't paying attention and got killed by that car. Not mine.

Ugh, would you just go away already? I'm too tired for this... I have class in the morning... I just want to sleep...

Listen, I'm not gonna kill myself, and I'm definitely not gonna "make love with you as a ghost over my own corpse." That's morbid and creepy.

No, I don't think it would be fun! Not to mention, I'm sure many other ghosts have already tried it.

Ghost Lady! (Exhale)

Ghost Lady... if I'm dead, the last thing I'm gonna think about is sex.

Now would you please... Get out of my bedroom!

(Exhale) Now I can get some rest... I hope she doesn't come back...

Number 13: Noisy Upstairs Neighbors Take a Shower

Time Length: 60 seconds

Categories/ Theme: Humorous, Slice of Life, Frustration, Conflict, Situational

Scene: A new tenant is sitting in their apartment. The building is old so they can hear everything that is going on upstairs.

It's so noisy here! I couldn't wait to move into my first apartment, but now it's my absolute worst nightmare! I can hear everything that my neighbors are doing!

Ugh! Looks like my moment of peace is over... They're home again... Stomp, stomp, stomp, creak, creak, creak! It just doesn't stop!

SIT DOWN ALREADY! Oh my gosh...

All I wanted to do was move out of my parent's house and now I feel like I'm being tortured.

Ugh... Now someone is taking a shower! It's so loud, I literally feel like I'm in the shower with them!

There has to be something I can do to drown out the noise! I can't just live like this...

(Step on wet carpet)

Huh? Why is my carpet wet? No way! Did their shower leak into my apartment???

Number 14: I'll Give You a Warning

Time Length: 60 seconds

Categories/ Theme: Humorous, Law, Slice of Life, Investigation, Authority

Scene: A police officer pulls over a driver for a headlight.

Missing headlight. Okay. Gonna pull this one over. Turn on the lights.

(Pause)

Well, looks like their blinker works. They're pulling up into the abandoned gas station. Okay, nice. I don't need to worry about oncoming traffic for this stop.

(Getting out of the cop car)

Yeesh... Can you say beater?

(Holding a flashlight to the window of the car pulled over)

"Does the window go down?"

(Pause)

"Okay, good. Do you know why I pulled you over? Your passenger side headlight is off. Oh, you have it in the car? So your dad was supposed to fix it? I see, you've been begging him to take care of it. Can I see your license and registration? Okay, thank you. I'll be right back."

(Walking back to the cop car)

Seems like a sweet lady. Her paperwork is current, good. She wasn't speeding. She has a good record. Last ticket was quite a while ago. Seems like an honest lady.

I don't really want to give her a ticket. The headlight was sitting on the seat. Plus the car is clearly old, so I don't think she needs a new financial burden right now. Maybe a warning will get her dad in gear.

(Getting out of the cop car and handing the warning to the driver)

Okay, I'm gonna give you a warning for now. Just go straight home and you can show this to your dad.

Drive safe now. Thank you, ma'am. You're awfully sweet. Have a good night.

Number 15: Don't You Come in Here

Time Length: 60 seconds

Categories/ Theme: Humorous, Slice of Life, Relationships, Communication, Overhearing

Scene: A downstairs tenant is trying to read but the upstairs neighbor comes home.

Ah, glad it's quiet tonight. Maybe I can actually read a full chapter without interrupt–

Ugh... Spoke too soon... Sounds like my neighbor just came home. Stomp, stomp, stomp up the stairs... WALK LIKE NORMAL PEOPLE, THUNDER FOOT!

(Pause)

Okay, sounds like he took off his shoes. Phew...

(Pause)

Oh? Did I just hear his girlfriend tell him, 'Don't you come in here'? Oo, he stayed out too late with the boys. He's in trouble.

(Pause)

Sounds like he's moving furniture around. Squeaky is mad—mad at him today, and he knows it too! He didn't even put up much of a fight. He's just gonna sleep on the couch. I guess it doesn't matter if it's his apartment, she's the boss.

(Pause, sigh)

I really don't need to know this much about my neighbors... I told the maintenance guys there wasn't enough sound reduction...

'Don't you come in here.'

(Bitter laugh)

How ridiculous! I can't believe I can hear that... Clear as day too.

(Sigh)

I need a new apartment...but it's too expensive to move... Ugh...

(Pause)

Well, Sounds like they went to bed... Back to my book.

Number 16: When Your Boss Wants You to Put Out a Fire

Time Length: 60 seconds

Categories/ Theme: Humorous, Workplace, Conflict, Frustration, Misunderstanding

Scene: An employee is telling her own father about an incident with her boss. He gets upset at her.

Hey Dad, how are you? My day was awful. My boss just kept yelling at me for every little thing I did wrong. Some of the stuff she was screaming about made no sense!

No, listen, this was over the top. She got upset because I didn't follow her instructions perfectly. I misunderstood one step, and she blew it out of proportion.

Then she started catastrophizing about a situation involving a fire. A fire! Dad, she expects me to help her put it out if, God forbid, something catches on fire! For minimum wage, I think she's asking far beyond my pay grade! If there was a fire at work, I would grab my keys and leave!

Whoa! Chill! Yes, I know getting out of the building is the priority, but I'm not gonna loiter next to my car with my fuming boss standing there blaming everything on me. No way! I'd tell her, "Consider this my two weeks' notice," and just leave!

Ugh... On that note, I'm going to start searching for a new job. Maybe something where the boss doesn't think I'm a firefighter on minimum wage.

Number 17: That's Because It's Not...

Time Length: 60 seconds

Categories/ Theme: Humorous, Slice of Life, Shopping, Food

Scene: A person just came back from the grocery store and wants to try out a new treat that was purchased there. This person is lactose intolerant.

Okay. I put all the stuff away. The only thing left is this baklava I got from the bakery. It wasn't the cheapest thing, but the label said it's lactose-free, and it looks so unbelievably good! I don't always get to enjoy all the treats I want because of this allergy, so it's really hard for me to say no...

I can't wait! I gotta try it now!

(Open the package and take a bite)

(Squirm with absolute delight because it's the best thing that you've ever tasted)

Oh my gosh! It's so sweet! The honey just saturates your mouth! It's so moist! Almost to the point of being mushy, but not quite there yet! And the crunchiness of the pistachios! It literally brings the perfect balance to the whole thing! Every bite is just as exquisite as the next! I could just cry! This might be the best thing that I've ever eaten!

Is this really lactose free? No way it is...

(read the package)

Doesn't say there's milk in the allergy section, but it doesn't list the ingredients either... That's odd...

It really doesn't taste lactose free. Oh! Here's the ingredients on the front of the packaging... Butter... That's why it doesn't taste lactose free... Because it's not...

(pause for the laugh)

Better go take a lactose pill now...

Number 18: New Jerseyans Don't Pump Gas

Time Length: 60 seconds

Categories/ Theme: Humorous, Cultural, Misunderstanding, Travel

Scene: Friend from New Jersey informs friend from another location that they somehow screwed up buying gas.

Hey, Buddy, um, next time I come visit you, I think maybe you should drive.

Oh, no! We didn't get into an accident or anything. It's quite easy to drive around here, actually.

The issue is what to do when we need gas. You see, in New Jersey, we have gas station attendants to pump the gas for us. It's actually illegal for us to pump gas in the State of New Jersey. And after what happened, I think there's a good reason why New Jerseyans don't pump their own gas.

So, we pull up to this gas station, and I hand my partner my card. He insists he can pump it himself, and I believe him. We fill the tank up without any issues. We're feeling pretty proud of ourselves for figuring it out... until I check my credit card statement later.

I don't see a charge for the gas. I'm positive I gave him the correct card. So what I'm saying is... we stole gas. We didn't mean to, but we sorta did...

(Pause, then with a mix of embarrassment and amusement)

So yeah... I'll give you cash. And maybe next time, I'll just stick to being a passenger!

Number 19: One Bag, Got It?

Time Length: 60 seconds

Categories/ Theme: Humorous, Introspective, Shopping, Slice of Life, Food

Scene: A person is going to the grocery store, but trying to remind themself to stay within a budget.

Okay. Before we go inside the store, Taylor, we need to have a quick conversation.

One bag only! Just one bag! That's all you're allowed to buy.

Remember, we're on a meal plan because cooking is not our thing, and the food is way better than what we can make.

But that meal plan isn't cheap—it takes up our whole food budget for the week.

We can only buy snacks at the store. Snacks and drinks.

One bag... We're here for milk and cereal. Anything else? It must fit in that bag or we walk away.

We spent too much last month, and we want new clothes next month. Got it?

One bag... One bag...

Okay! I can do this! I'm not going to buy too much! I got this!

(Starts heading to the store)

(Turns around)

But maybe I'll bring the bigger bag... just in case there's a sale or something.

Number 20: Featured from Over My Dead Body, Volume 2: Chapter 7

Time Length: 60 seconds

Categories/ Theme: Humorous, Supernatural, Horror, Exorcism, Afterlife

Scene: An exorcist communicates with Mayumi then relays what she has seen to Hiroki.

Oh. OH! WHAT PAIN! METAL COLLIDING INTO MY SOFT FLESH! WHERE IS THAT GUY? WHICH WAY DID HE GO? WHERE DID HE GO?

OH! Oh. Ah...

(The exorcist, speaking to Hiroki)

The spirits have brought me Mayumi's final moments. It seems she got distracted while following you and was hit by a car. In her last moments, her mind fixated on finding you, and that thought carried into the spirit realm, causing her to forget everything else about her life and to latch onto some... truly unholy desires.

What can you do to stop her? There isn't much I can do for you. Mayumi isn't a bad spirit, but she's become an angry one—upset about her untimely death and feeling that she missed out on something in life. The only way to send Mayumi to the light is to give her what she wants.

Think carefully, Hiroki. Try to figure out what Mayumi truly desires beneath her obsession with you.

Number 21: You were Jealous?

Time Length: 60 seconds

Categories/ Theme: Dramatic, Relationships, Misunderstanding, Self-Discovery, Thoughtful

Scene: Two people discuss a past experience over being jealous of each other.

You were jealous of me? Really? I was jealous of you! Of course I was! I wanted to do what you were doing!

You thought I was trying to steal your role? No! I didn't mean to make you feel that way! I couldn't steal it even if I wanted to. They definitely liked you more than me. When I tried to make suggestions for someone else, they told me to focus on my own role. They were probably right; I was a newbie and should have kept quiet.

Oh, that? I wasn't trying to outdo you! I was using you as a benchmark to compete with myself.

See, you already won! You were picked as the best! I wanted to learn from you so I could do better for my next opportunity. I never meant to make you feel insecure.

But hey, I'll take that as a compliment. And honestly, I was jealous of you too. But I never would have acted on it because it's my responsibility to keep my feelings in check.

Oh, I wish you'd brought this up sooner. We could have worked it out right away.

Thank you for telling me now, though. I'm sorry we had this experience. I hope we don't have to be jealous of each other anymore. We're teammates from now on!

Number 22: News Anchor

Time Length: 60 seconds

Categories/Theme: Dramatic, Social Commentary, Ethics, Afterlife, Technology, Thoughtful

Scene: News Anchor goes over ground breaking technology.

And our top story tonight: Reincarnation is real, and now you can find out who you once were in another life. Thanks to PasLi Co's revolutionary device, the Past Defirer, we can now see every human life a soul has lived. People from all walks of life are lining up to discover their past identities, eager to uncover the secrets of their souls.

But this breakthrough comes with unexpected consequences. Criminal justice representatives are lobbying Congress to mandate past life checks for all citizens. Their goal? To identify anyone who committed crimes in previous lives without fully serving their sentences.

The question on everyone's mind: Could you be a criminal and not even know it? In just the past three days, the Past Defirer has uncovered nearly 30 individuals who died before completing their jail sentences in past lives. These cases are now being retried in modern courts, with good behavior in this lifetime factoring into the final verdicts.

As we grapple with these unprecedented ethical dilemmas, one can't help but wonder: How will this reshape our understanding of justice, identity, and personal responsibility? And more importantly, are we ready for the truths the Past Defirer might reveal about ourselves and our loved ones?

Stay tuned for our exclusive interview with Dr. Marcus and Marissa Chekno, husband and wife lead developers of the Past Defirer, as we explore the far-reaching implications of this groundbreaking technology.

Number 23: The Other Mermaid

Time Length: 60 seconds

Categories/ Theme: Introspective, Dramatic, Self-Discovery, Fantasy, Romance

Scene: A mermaid was discovered by the human that she had a crush on. Now she is processing her fears while grappling with an argument with her mother forbidding her from falling in love with a human.

Where can I go now? What can I do? I can't go home after what happened with Mother, but I can't go back to Nate either! He knows who I am now! He knows my secret!

Mother never told me to not come home. It's already been weeks since I've last seen her. I'm sure she's not mad at me anymore.

But I'm still mad at her! Nothing will ever change if I return! She will continue to push me into going on dates I never wanted and scold me about sins I've never committed.

But haven't I committed those sins by now? Mother was always worried that I would fall in love with a human. Can I even say that I haven't?

Love is such a strong word. I've only talked to Nate a few times. Just because I sang him to sleep those few nights doesn't mean I'm in love with him.

Then why did I do it?

Because I found him interesting, nothing more. It doesn't even matter now. I know he doesn't want to see me anymore.

He never actually said that, did he? He only acknowledged that I was a mermaid. I left before he even had a chance to form an opinion.

It doesn't matter! Humans and mermaids don't belong together. I'm certain he knows this!

I should know that too...

Number 24: Six Month Anniversary

Time Length: 60 seconds

Categories/Theme: Wistful, Humorous, Romance, Relationships, Daydreaming, Love

Scene: A young woman is preparing a picnic for her boyfriend to celebrate their 6 month anniversary. She is in her kitchen gushing to herself about how they met.

Hmm, hm, hm, hm. There! It's all set! Oh, I can't wait for George to see what I've made for our special day! It's our six-month anniversary, and I want it to be unforgettable. I can't believe how quickly time has passed already! Soon it will be our one year... then our two years... and who knows? Maybe he'll propose! Before we know it, it'll be our wedding day! And then it'll be our six-year anniversary! Then maybe our sixtieth!

Oh, slow down time! Let me take a moment to enjoy this! That's why I've decided to fill my basket with all the things he loves to eat and surprise him at his door. I can't slow down time, but I can definitely savor each moment!

I can't believe it was only six months ago that I was wandering the woods and stumbled upon his house. He scared me with those hedge clippers! I was afraid he was a crazy attacker, but no—just a geeky little PhD making his late uncle's former home look presentable. I was so taken aback by his handiness and intelligence; I could talk to him for hours.

Oh! Time is flying by again! Mustn't be late! See you later, big empty home!

Number 25: Let Me Reintroduce Myself

Time Length: 60 seconds

Categories/ Theme: Wistful, Family, Thoughtful, Childhood, Communication

Scene: A cousin reintroduces herself to her cousin's young children who are uncomfortable because they never see her. She later turns to the mother of the children to tell her why she reintroduces herself to the kids.

(To the kids)

I know, you don't remember me and that's okay. I didn't remember all of my relatives when I was your age either. You're probably going to forget me the next time you see me too. That's why every time I see you, I'm going to reintroduce myself. I'm cousin Jessie. I grew up with your mommy and aunts and uncle. I promise to do this every time I see you. All you need to know is I'm family and I love you both very much. One day, you will appreciate this.

(Switch to the adults around them)

When I was little, my family members from my father's side would just assume that I knew who they were, and it was very awkward for me. It was hard for me to connect with them because I couldn't remember them. Then one of my extended cousins actually reintroduced herself.

From then on, I felt much more at ease around her. Then I was able to relax around the other cousins too. Now I'm able to enjoy spending time with my extended family.

That's what I want for the girls—I want them to feel comfortable with me. And I'll keep reintroducing myself until one day, I won't have to anymore.

Number 26: Featured from My First Manga: Ryuu Romance

Time Length: 60 seconds

Categories/ Theme: Wistful, Romance, Dramatic, Self-Discovery, Love

Scene: Two lovers separated by a waterfall meet in secret every morning.

In the morning, I heard him call out to me. I dashed to the waterfall that separated us. I couldn't let the others hear him. "Taiyo?" I asked. He responded by leaping toward me, but I quickly put my hands out to stop him.

"You'll get wet," I said to him, "And then the others will know that you were here."

Before I could follow up with an apology, I heard the sound of a zipper. Then moments later, his face emerged from the waterfall barrier.

He looked into my eyes and said, "I don't care." Then without warning, he kissed me. I was shocked but I kissed him back. I never kissed a boy before. Had I known that he was going to kiss me then and there, I would have been so nervous, but once our lips met, I didn't feel that way at all.

When we finally parted he said that he would return tomorrow then disappeared behind the waterfall. And he did return the next day and the day after that. Each time, he'd kiss me, proving to me that it wasn't a dream. I really did have my first kiss! Best of all, it was with him!

A week went by and we did this every morning. That is until the waterfall froze solid. With our passageway sealed off, all we could see of one another was a distorted reflection. Only a peak...

90-Second Monologues

Number 27: Widow on her Wedding Day

Time Length: 90 seconds

Categories/ Theme: Dramatic, Supernatural, Fantasy, Conflict, Revenge, Afterlife

Scene: A demonic, ghostly wizard like creature reveals his backstory

So you've finally figured out how to find me. Very good. Does that mean you remember me now?

Of course not! How could you? That was lifetimes ago! You were reborn, having no idea why I've come to kill you. We've done this dance how many times now? Six, seven? Each time, I disintegrated your body into ash in an instant, leaving you clueless about what happened—or why it happened.

But this time was different. This time, you survived my attack. Do you know why you didn't turn to dust this time?

Yes, your husband took your place. He stepped in front of you, so when I reached out my hand, he disintegrated instead. Because he no longer existed, I could not take my revenge on you this time. His death meant that you were no longer married; therefore, our vow was not violated anymore.

Confused? Well, many lifetimes ago, you chose to marry me! You vowed your soul to me, and I intended to keep it that way forever.

But you betrayed me. You used our marriage as a ploy to get close to me—to destroy me. You knew I was planning to enslave all of humanity and kill anyone who resisted. You knew I would have a soft spot for my spouse.

I loved you, but I was no fool! I put a curse on you during our vows so that if you ever betrayed me, I would haunt you and destroy you in every lifetime thereafter. The curse, of course, is activated by marriage.

So now you know why you became a widow on your wedding day.

Number 28: Featured from Powerless the Opening of the Story

Time Length: 90 seconds

Categories/ Theme: Dramatic, Fantasy, Introspective, Family, Self-Discovery

Scene: A family member describes how his life as an ordinary person is like in a household full of sorcerers.

It sucks to be left out. Whether it's being picked last for a sporting game or not being invited to a big party, everyone knows that empty feeling of, "What about me? Can't I come too?" For most people, this isn't a big deal for very long. But for me, this is my entire life.

I feel left out by the people around me every single day. Every second, I sit back and watch as my brother, sister, and parents do the impossible—they use magic. All of them are so skilled, so amazing. We share the same blood, yet I can't even make a tiny flame flicker between my fingers.

During a blackout, I'm stuck in the dark. When I lose something, it takes me days to find it. If I'm running late, I just have to accept being late. Meanwhile, my family solves everything with a simple snap, a wave of their hand, or just by closing their eyes.

It makes me feel so small, so inadequate. Jealousy isn't even the right word anymore—it's a deep, constant ache of being the one who doesn't belong. Just once, I'd love to snap my fingers and light a candle like everyone else in my family. Just once, I want to feel what it's like to not be... ordinary.

Why did I have to be the unlucky one? Why did I have to be born powerless?

Number 29: Traitor to the Republic

Time Length: 90 seconds

Categories/ Theme: Dramatic, Historical Fiction, Emotional, Imprisonment

Scene: A prisoner from the Reign of Terror is called for execution.

Hear that? The guards are coming. Their boots echo in the corridor. It's not meal time, so it must mean they're taking another poor soul to the guillotine.

Come here. Let us pray. Pray that they pass us by. Pray that this nightmare ends and no one else has to face Madam de Guillotine. Pray we will see another dawn and taste freedom once more. Pray—

Oh no... Did they just say my name? Did you hear it? No... it can't be! Perhaps they meant Céleste Dupont, not Céleste Dupuis! This cannot be happening.

No... no... Please don't open that door! I want to stay here! Can't I stay here? Please! Just let me remain in this shadowed corner! I'll be a good prisoner! I'll do anything—anything! Just please—

Why won't you say anything? How can you stand there silently while I plead for my life? Am I no longer human? Is that it? Do you see me as nothing more than an object, a thing that makes incoherent noises from time to time?

Why me? Why must I go? What have I done? I wasn't even told what my crime was before they threw me in here! Why am I labeled an enemy of the state? How am I a traitor to the French Republic?

I haven't done anything! I'm innocent! Please, stop! Don't take me away!

Number 30: Good Dog Goes Bad

Time Length: 90 seconds

Categories/ Theme: Dramatic, Supernatural, Horror, Transformation, Tragedy

Scene: A dog owner relays to the Police a Supernatural incident involving her dog.

It was a normal day at the park with friends and my little brother. We brought our dog, Timmy, with us—a big, happy puppy. He was leashed and excited for an adventure.

When my friends arrived—George, Helen, Jennifer, Denice, Benedict, Nathan, Gleb, and Sam—it was a big group. They'd all met Timmy before. Helen and Jennifer had just slept over last week. We all slept in the living room with Timmy snuggling up in the blankets beside us, snoring loudly.

But today... Timmy suddenly slipped his collar. I called out, expecting him to bow his head like usual whenever I scolded him. Instead, he turned and... growled. The sound was deep, guttural—wrong. His eyes changed from soft brown to an eerie fluorescent yellow.

"Timmy?" I asked. My friends grew quiet, fixated on his sudden change.

Then he lunged at Helen. We were shocked, frozen. She screamed—then stopped as Timmy went for her throat. Helen was the first to die...

We all started running. George tried to help Helen; Timmy took him out next. Then Denice. Ben fought with a stick but lost. Then Jennifer...

You said my other friends and little brother escaped? They're okay? That's good...

And Timmy? Gone...

I'm sorry, Officers; this is all I know. My Timmy was a loving and sweet dog. I don't understand what happened. It wasn't natural. Something took over him.

I fear it could happen again. Will there be an investigation into what caused this?

Number 31: A Good Snap

Time Length: 90 seconds

Categories/ Theme: Dramatic, Suspense, Psychological, Imprisonment, Breaking Point

Scene: An innocent person is in prison and reflects on where they are. Then abruptly snaps.

I've been a good person all my life. In school, I got good grades. I never picked fights, even when I was bullied. I went to a good college, got what people call a "good job." I did everything right.

So how did I end up here... in prison? Charged with a crime I didn't commit. Stripped of my clothes, my dignity. No trial yet, but somehow I'm denied bail. I have the money! I've always been responsible. Why is this happening? Why was my freedom taken from me? How could anyone think I'd do something like this?

(Notices someone looking)

What? Why are you staring? What do you want?

(Catches self, voice lowering)

No, I didn't mean to... I'm not looking for trouble. I'm not like these criminals—I don't belong here. I'm a good person, I swear!

(Panic rising)

Oh no. I showed weakness, didn't I? They're coming closer. What do I do? Stand down? Try to stay invisible? Run to a guard?

(Pause, then with growing intensity)

No. No more. I'm done being good! What has 'good' ever gotten me?

(A slow, unsettling smile spreads across face)

All my life, I've grinned and borne everything. Tried not to snap. Played by the rules.

Not anymore...

(Standing, voice rising as they flip the chair)

WHAT THE F*CK DO YOU WANT?

Number 32: No Teeth...

Time Length: 90 seconds

Categories/ Theme: Dramatic, Workplace, Emotional, Self-Discovery, Anxiety

Scene: A worker has a meltdown about her job.

I can't do this job anymore! I hate it! I can't handle how early it starts! And my boss wants me to work more hours! I'm supposed to be a part-time employee! If I work more hours, it's like being forced to work full-time without the benefits!

I've been there for over two years last Tuesday, and instead of giving me a review, she picked apart every little thing I did! I could do absolutely nothing right! By the end of my shift, I wanted to climb into the dumpster because I felt like garbage! I think she just didn't want to give me a raise!

And the patients? Some are great, but the mean ones are just awful! I made a mistake because of my eye issue, and one lady accused me of discrimination! She didn't even let me explain! I hate her—not because I'm racist, but because she unfairly labeled me when I was just trying to help her save money!

My jaw has been hurting me so badly from all the stress! I think I'm grinding my teeth! I can't believe I'm so stressed out that I'm gonna lose my teeth from grinding them so hard! Then I'm gonna lose my job because...

(Start to really cry here) I work in a dental office!

...No one wants to go to a dentist where the front desk girl has no teeth...

What am I going to do? Find another job? Who would hire me?!

Number 33: Let There be Rain

Time Length: 90 seconds

Categories/Theme: Dramatic, Humorous, Situational, Friendship, Conflict

Scene: She is angry at her friend. They had plans but she decides not to go because the friend makes him/ her angry. She enters angrily and complains about the friend.

I can't believe she told me not to come! I'm the problem here? Seriously? Last time we went to the beach, her stupid friends made us wait for them for two hours! Two hours! Yet, she wants me to be ready to go by 7:30 AM! For what? So we can sit in the parking lot for two hours again?

Ugh, why is she always forcing me to get up so early? I keep telling her I can't do it! Why is she so mean to me? How could she choose them over me?

Wouldn't it be great if it rained tomorrow...

It would be super sunny and look totally perfect all the way there. They arrive at the beach and pay to get in. They set up their blankets, chairs, umbrellas...put the cooler in the shade... Just as they sit down, soak up the sun, open up a nice cold Pepsi... I know that bitch is gonna drink Pepsi. Cream soda is way better on the beach, or a Mikes Hard lemonade, but no, she's gonna have Pepsi.

Right as it hits her lips, clouds start rolling in. The wind picks up; they'll have to grab their jackets—but they'll forget them in the car! Just as they huddle together for warmth, the rain starts pouring down—freezing drops chilling their spines! The wind knocks over their umbrellas; one flies away!

The gray clouds stretch on for miles as they gather their things and return to the car totally soaked. They sit there for fifteen minutes, shivering, when suddenly they see a ray of hope! They get out of the car thinking it's cleared—only for the rain to start again, soaking them to the bone!

Oh wouldn't it be wonderful if it rained?

Number 34: Extractions

Time Length: 90 seconds

Categories/ Theme: Dramatic, Medical, Ethics, Health

Scene: A patient coordinator shares a concern with her employer, the general dentist.

"Excuse me, Doctor. I have a concern about your next patient. He told me that tomorrow he's scheduled for an extraction of six permanent teeth! I looked at his chart and I don't see anything suggesting those teeth are unhealthy.

I know I'm only at the front desk, but I can't understand why this patient would need so many teeth removed! He takes really good care of his oral health. His last cavity was years ago too. Am I out of line here, or is this really unusual?

The only thing I saw in your chart is that he might have an issue with crowding. It would make sense if he was getting his wisdom teeth removed, but all the teeth scheduled for removal are second molars and two first molars! There's no way his mouth is that crowded, right? I've never heard of something like this before. I'm just in shock! How could a physician even think to do this to such a young guy? He has so much of his life ahead of him to just lose so many of his teeth!

Oh, right. You said Oral Surgeons only have one thing on their minds... extract, extract, extract. I still think a reasonable person shouldn't put a patient so young in a situation like this.

Oh, good! You agree! Thank you, Doctor. I know I may have crossed a line by bringing this up, but I just wanted to tell you in case it didn't come to your attention during the appointment. I'm so relieved you'll look into it. I'll send him in now. Thanks again for listening.

Number 35: Featured from Future Project: Dating AI

Time Length: 90 seconds

Categories/ Theme: Dramatic, Sci-fi, Romance, Technology, Ethics

Scene: A woman caught her datable robot beating up her boyfriend and explains to him why she doesn't need him anymore.

No! Stop!

Please don't hurt him anymore! Can't you see he's unconscious?

Kolby, listen to me. You've done everything I've asked. You've been everything I wanted. But that doesn't change the facts. You didn't do these things because you wanted to. You did them because you were programmed to. You're a robot, Kolby.

I know you're saying you're programmed to want to do everything with me. And you've done such a great job. You've helped me through an awful time in my life. You've stood by me, helped me succeed. But now... I don't need you anymore. And I'm so sorry.

I was going to do right by you, Kolby. Find you a nice new home, someone else who needed you. We'd wipe your programming so you could be their perfect person, be happy with them.

I know you keep saying you want to be with me, but that's your programming talking. With just a few button presses, you'd forget all about me. You could help someone who truly needs you.

So please, don't hurt him anymore. Don't hurt the one I love. Let me call an ambulance. We'll take him to the hospital, and when we come back, we can find you a new home.

You want to know why I'd choose him over you? Why I'm protecting him now? Even though we might disagree and fight, even though he's been married before and has children?

Because given the choice between a perfect lie and something real and true, people will always pick the real one. You, Kolby, can give me everything but one thing - the one thing that truly matters. A human connection.

Kolby, no! Please don't shoot!

Number 36: Get Out!

Time Length: 90 seconds

Categories/ Theme: Dramatic, Relationships, Empowerment, Abuse, Overcoming Adversity

Scene: An abuse victim of her spouse finally stands up to him after 16 years.

No!

[PAUSE]

You heard me, I said no. Don't you dare come any closer to me! And shut up! It's my turn to speak! Shut it!

For sixteen years, I listened to you. I believed you knew best. Trusted you had our best interests at heart. But now I see it clearly: I was never part of that "best interest." I was just a tool for you, a lesser being meant to serve your so-called greatness.

You convinced me I was too naive to make my own decisions. That I couldn't be trusted. I never wanted to be a stay-at-home mom, but you made me believe that all we needed was your income. And only you needed a car. I could just take a bicycle until you got home. I studied business, yet somehow, because you brought in the money, you controlled how we spent it.

But you listen to me! You are not smarter than me! You think you are, but you're not!

You studied history, yet you believe we were better off under monarchies. Monarchies! As if the wars and suffering they caused never happened. How could you have studied history for four years and not know that?

Gah! How was I so blind to your ignorance? You liked monarchies because you wanted to wear the crown yourself—like a king! News flash: You're not! You're nothing!

I don't need to listen to you anymore! I refuse to listen to you ever again! I want you to leave! Get out!

Number 37: I Didn't Know

Time Length: 90 seconds

Categories/ Theme: Dramatic, Relationships, Introspective, Abuse, Self-Discovery, Overcoming Adversity

Scene: A young woman explains her sexual experience with her abusive ex boyfriend.

[Content Warning: This monologue contains references to sexual coercion and non-consensual situations.]

The first time my ex tried to be intimate, he forced himself on me. We were in his bed, watching TV, relaxed. Suddenly, he became aggressive, taking off his shirt and kissing me all over. I didn't like it. I just wanted to cuddle and watch TV. His parents were right outside the door.

I was still a virgin, confused about what was happening. Every time, he was trying to have sex. I kept telling myself I should want it because I loved him, but I didn't. It makes me sick thinking about it now.

I'd talk about anything to turn him off - my parents, his parents, even describing someone with "candy corn teeth." I was trying to help him not feel so horny. But he didn't want any help with that. He wanted to be horny. He wanted to have sex. He described it like being hungry and the only way to stop being hungry was to eat.

Eventually, the only way to stop him was to cry. It was the only thing that made his arousal go away. I convinced myself it was my fault, my anxiety preventing me from wanting it.

He used to shame me for not wanting sex, but it was clearly one-sided from the start. I understand now that my feelings didn't matter to him. There was no love in this. I'm learning to trust my feelings and set boundaries. No one should ever feel pressured into unwanted intimacy.

I'm sharing this to help others. Remember, it's okay to be alone, and you don't owe anyone sex. I hope my story shows that's the truth.

Number 38: Why Can't I Just Say No?

Time Length: 90 seconds

Categories/ Theme: Dramatic, Relationships, Introspective, Social Commentary, Empowerment

Scene: A woman turns a guy down and returns to her friend. Her friend is pressuring her to go on a date even though she's not interested and this makes her mad.

Oh him? He just asked me out for coffee. I declined though.

Because I'm in love with someone else.

Yeah, I know he doesn't even know I exist, but I still want him.

What about that guy just now?

He's alright, I guess, but he's not my type. Look, just because someone offers doesn't mean I have to accept. I don't need to be in a relationship to be happy.

You know, why is it that I have to always feel bad for turning a guy down? Like it's expected that I should give him a chance just to prove that I'm a nice person. I am a nice person. Letting a guy that I'm not attracted to take me out on a date just doesn't seem like a nice thing to do. We'd just be wasting both of our time.

And like I said, I have feelings for someone else. I told him that, and he was fine with it.

Don't give me that! I'm not interested in dating him so I told him the truth: I like someone else. That should be a good enough excuse.

Why do women even have to make an excuse to say no anyway? Why should anyone? How about, "No?" Just, "No thank you." Or a "I appreciate your offer but it's a no." Then we can all move on with our lives.

Honestly, my dating life is none of your business—or anyone's. I didn't ask for your help, and I'd rather wait for the guy I truly want. After all, I only get one romantic partner. Why should I settle for anyone else?

I'm really waiting for someone special. If the guy I like ever notices me, that would be great. If he doesn't, we can all move on to other people.

Number 39: Why Would You Watch This Garbage?

Time Length: 90 seconds

Categories/ Theme: Dramatic, Relationships, Conflict, Abuse, Manipulation

Scene: A controlling partner berates his partner at an airport

Still an hour before we can board... I can't wait to go home... What are you doing, kitten? Ugh! You're watching that again? Seriously? Why?

You like that crap? You think those people are cool? They are not cool! They're losers! None of them have any talent! I can't believe you would watch this crap! This is such a waste of time! It's so stupid!

Why am I getting so angry? Because you chose to waste your time watching garbage! There are so many different things we could be doing and you're choosing to watch trash on Youtube!

So what if we're in the airport! That's no reason to sit around watching garbage! I just don't understand what you even like about this crap! It's all fake!

Not all of it? Not all of it! You're so dumb sometimes! Not all of it...

What's my problem? I don't have a problem! I just want you to realize that all that crap you watch on Youtube is dumb and you shouldn't watch it anymore!

I wish you would take how you spend your time more seriously. You could be reading something or playing a game or I don't know, talking about something more engaging.

You just want to relax and watch your stupid videos... Fine... Watch your fake, garbage, bullshit videos then. You do that... Just keep acting like you don't care at all...

(Look at imaginary partner and walk off in a huff)

Number 40: Why Is He Crying?

Time Length: 90 seconds

Categories/ Theme: Dramatic, Relationships, Introspective, Conflict, Ambition

Scene: A partner reacts to her boyfriend's tears in an unusual way. She reflects on it

Why... Why is he crying?

My boyfriend is literally crying in front of me, yet I don't feel the empathy I usually do. I don't have the urge to comfort him or hold him. No... I feel disgusted.

He asked me what I wanted out of life. He always likes to dig deep into my feelings whenever he smokes weed. It often feels like a drill into my psyche, and it doesn't feel good. He always asks me to justify my answers, which is hard for me to articulate. If I can't convince him that my reasoning is good enough, it feels like whatever I'm feeling is dismissed.

I told him I want to become a published author and build a company that makes a huge profit. Why? Because I don't want to work a regular job, and I want the world to see how talented I am.

That's when he started crying. Most people in my life love that I'm ambitious like this. But somehow, my partner—the man I considered marrying one day—finds this to be something worth crying about?

He told me he feels sorry for me. Sorry for me? This is what I've always wanted, and I'm working to achieve it! Other people around the world say they want to follow their dreams but don't, and they're miserable. I don't want to be one of those people.

When I asked what he wants out of life, he just sniveled, "I want to be happy." But how does my pursuit of my dreams not contribute to that? He's still crying, and I'm still... disgusted.

Is this normal? I don't know...

Number 41: The Sandbox

Time Length: 90 seconds

Categories/ Theme: Dramatic, Relationships, Conflict, Emotional, Frustration

Scene: A person reflects on a fight with an ex.

I'll never forget this fight that I had with my ex. It was very unlike me.

We were in the process of moving in together, so he bought a house near his work. Only problem was it was two hours from my job, so I couldn't officially move in until I got a new one.

It was on a day that I'd finished working for the week, and I was going to spend the next couple days at what we were calling "our" house. I stopped at my parents' home to change and grab some things then drove forty-five minutes to "our" house.

The drive there was long and irritating, and I was already crabby from working and having to get up earlier than usual on a Saturday. It didn't help that the traffic was heavy either.

When I arrived at "our" house, all I wanted to do was pull into the driveway. But my ex took up the whole thing with his car and a sandbox left behind from the previous owners. This meant there was no room for my car.

I had asked my ex to please leave space for me in the driveway when I first arrived so parking would be easier for me, but he apparently did not think it was worth doing that one little thing for me!

Trying not to get too angry, I called him and asked if he could park my car on the street so I didn't have to.

He answered with an agitated, "Oh my gosh! Learn to park!" Which made me furious!

I hung up the phone, cautiously parked on the street, walked straight to the driveway to pick up the sandbox, and then threw it across the lawn!

Then I went into my ex's house and gave him an earful. He left for the rest of the day after our fight, which made me feel relieved. I made my point, and I got the whole house to myself for hours. Peace at last.

Number 42: Darby, I'm Furious

Time Length: 90 seconds

Categories/ Theme: Humorous, Relationships, Situational, Frustration, Technology

*Scene: A spouse gets a call from his spouse's cell phone regarding the landline phone. He still has one for some reason and gets overly upset whenever it's unplugged. *Remember to get ridiculously angry for this piece.*

Hello, Darby? What's going on? I called the home phone, and no one answered. You did what?!

You unplugged the phone? Why? Why would you do that? You know you can't just unplug it like that! It reboots the whole system!

It doesn't matter if you plugged it back in! You know how that phone is! If you unplug it, it messes everything up, and we need to call the company to get it fixed! No! It doesn't reboot on its own! You know better!

Darby... Darby! Let me talk! Let–me–talk!

I am furious with you! I am just boiling! You have absolutely no idea what you've done! What could you possibly need to unplug the phone for? For your hair dryer? That was worth taking down the whole system? Darby, I am furious with you right now! No! Don't touch anything else until I get home! I am absolutely enraged with you right now!

You know how important it is for the home phone to work when the doctor calls! I don't understand why you would do that! I'm very disgusted with you! That was very, very bad!

Listen to me! You are going to call the company right now—let me finish! You're going to call them and fix this! I am so unbelievably angry right now that I can't even think straight!

Darby–Darby...

(Take in an angry breath)

Darby. Darby! Listen to me right now! You have messed up very badly! I don't think you understand how serious this is! No! Call the company; I'm done talking to you! Goodbye!

Number 43: While the Whole World Slept

Time Length: 90 seconds

Categories/ Theme: Humorous, Sci-fi, Situational, Misunderstanding, Satire

Scene: An alien wants to destroy all the humans on Earth but makes a small miscalculation.

I've been studying the creatures of Earth for quite some time now, my lord. You see, the poison bomb my team has created could wipe out all the human creatures in one fell swoop. We just need every single one asleep. After extensive research, I discovered there's one moment every two and a half centuries when all human creatures will be unconscious for three minutes.

Today is that day! Just one bomb, and we can eliminate them all. These humans are savage, beastly creatures—smarter and deadlier than any other earthly beings. They'd kill us on sight!

(Turns to the lord)

You approve of our plan, my lord? Excellent! We shall watch from your monitor.

(Pause and come up with a quirky way to communicate with the team)

Launching in ten, nine—wait! NO! They're waking up early in Newfoundland! And the East Coast too where the wild Florida

Man resides! This can't be! Why would they wake up an hour early?

(Get a message from your team)

What?! Do you have information? Why are the human creatures waking up? Where did my calculations go wrong? I don't believe this! They call it "Daylight Saving Time!"

How could this be? The other side of Earth doesn't do this? Why do territories in the Northern Hemisphere do something so bizarre? How do they expect to save daylight like this?

My lord... it seems we cannot wipe out the humans today. Our next opportunity? Two hundred and fifty earthly years from now.

(Bows slightly, dejected)

I will see myself out.

Number 44: The Worst Pet

Time Length: 90 seconds

Categories/ Theme: Humorous, Relationships, Situational, Animal/Nature, Conflict

Scene: A spouse brings home a badger for a pet

My husband came home one day carrying a box and said, "Honey, c'mere! Check out my new pet!"

I was so excited. I thought, "Oh, finally! He's brought me a kitten or perhaps a puppy!"

No sooner did I approach the box than I heard the most ghoulish growl. Certainly not a kitten! So I asked him, "Honey? What is that?"

He opened the box, and there was a badger in there! I jumped back in alarm as the beast immediately poked its head out and stared at me, baring its teeth.

I screamed, "Honey! Put that down right now! That's not a cat! That's a wild animal!"

But he was completely calm and said, "Awe, he's just a little queasy from being in the box. He's really sweet. Give him a little pet."

I told him, "No thank you." Then my husband started heading toward our front door. I asked him, "Where do you think you're going?"

He said, "I'm gonna take Oreo into the living room for cuddles."

I exclaimed, "Absolutely not! Have you gone mad?"

He replied, "He'll warm up to you."

I insisted, "Let him stay in the barn until he does."

My husband was not pleased but he obeyed.

The very next day, the badger burrowed its way out of the barn—and thankfully we haven't seen it since!

Number 45: Cricket Flour Bread

Time Length: 90 seconds

Categories/ Theme: Humorous, Renaissance Faire, Situational, Conflict, Innovation, Historical Fiction

Scene: This is an argument between the miller and the baker during the Renaissance period. So, "thou," will be used instead of, "you." The miller invented cricket flour long before it was created in modern times.

Baker! Where is my cricket flour bread? Thou saidst thou wouldst have it all baked by Monday. It is now Tuesday! Where is it?

Thou baked one loaf? And? It was green? I care not what color it might be. Didst thou taste it? How did it taste? It tasted fine? Well, of course it did! All the flour that I mill makes fine bread!

Now where are the rest of the loaves? Thou threw them away? Why? I care not if they were green! The color matters not!

I told thee! My mother cannot eat bread! She gets bumps all over her body and nearly dies every time it happens. 'Tis a very uncomfortable experience for her. I'm a miller that cannot feed his own mother! 'Tis a tragedy! So I have been trying to find other ways to make bread for her!

How did I come up with cricket flour? Thou see, my cat loves crickets. He loves to chase them, pounce on them and bite them. But he does not eat them, so my floor is often littered with cricket corpses that I used to throw away. But one day, I got very busy and left the dead crickets on the windowsill. They ended up drying in the sun into perfectly dry husks. So I decided to run them through the mill and they ended up making a very palatable flour.

(Pauses briefly for reaction)

Which brings me to the here and now. I need the loaves that I requested. Surely, thou didst not throw all the dough that I left here away...

Well, if thou refusest to bake it, I suppose I must become both the miller and the baker! Out of my way! I will show thee how 'tis done!

Number 46: Paint and Sip

Time Length: 90 seconds

Categories/ Theme: Humorous, Situational, Friendship, Art, Communication

Scene: Two friends are at a paint and sip. One friend is absolutely terrible at painting and the main speaker is trying to spare her feelings.

Thank you for inviting me here. It's been really fun. I didn't know I could enjoy painting so much!

The wine choices are great too. Let me see what yours looks like so far.

Oh! Well, it seems you've taken some creative initiative. Were we supposed to include that line there? And that chair? Oh! Right! That's a dog. Of course it is.

(Takes a sip of the wine)

The wine is really great here.

Oh, you come here all the time? Every week? Wow... What do you do with all the paintings? You give them away to your friends? And do they like them?

I see. And they display them? In their homes, right?

Oh, that's too bad that you haven't been able to go visit. I'm sure they have your paintings displayed front and center in their living rooms.

Oh dear! No, I like mine just fine the way it is! You don't have to add the tree there... The instructor doesn't seem to have a tree in theirs... Right... Bob Ross.
(Takes a sip of wine)
Great wine.

Oh, you want to give me yours? You want me to display it? In my house? How thoughtful... Definitely gonna need more wine...

(Takes a sip)

You know what? Maybe I'll just hang it right next to my "masterpiece," in the basement. It'll be like an art gallery set aside specifically for these! That way we can make more and expand our collection!

Number 47: The Thoughtful Spider

Time Length: 90 seconds

Categories/ Theme: Humorous, Animal/Nature, Introspective, Slice of Life

Scene: A person casually and playfully talks to a spider that is on the front door.

Hello, little spider. I'm closing the door, so be careful of your legs.

You know why I'm being so nice to you? Earlier, when I entered my home, you fell off the door and into the foyer. I was very annoyed because I really didn't want you in my house. It's a big world out there; you can go anywhere outside! I hate when bugs—well, in your case, arachnids—come inside where I live.

But unlike most spiders, you decided to just walk outside the door. It was as if you knew you were in a place where you weren't wanted. You took the initiative to read the room, and I appreciate that.

I guess you just want to hang around outside the door. That's fine with me. You're outside and a harmless Daddy Longlegs. I don't have a problem sharing since you were respectful towards me.

My mother told me that I attract spiders because I'm a writer. I've been writing a lot lately, staying up late into the night. I'm not sure whether you spiders are helping me write or if I see more of you because you're attracted to my creativity. So, sorry about that—or thanks...

Man... I must be tired... I'm talking to a spider...

Well, see you later, my eight-legged friend...

Number 48: Gacies on a Stick

Time Length: 90 seconds

Categories/ Theme: Humorous, Thoughtful, Family, Informative, Cultural

Scene: A Polish American describes a linguistic observation about her heritage and describes a family phrase relating to it

My family is Polish. We came to the US around the 1880s, though I'm not sure of the exact year. It was a common time period for Polish immigrants to move to the US.

I believe my family arrived during what's called the second wave of Polish immigration. Interestingly, you can often tell the difference between first, second, and third-wave Polish-Americans by their use of two specific Polish words. One of these words is "Dupa." This word is still used in Poland today, but second-wave Polish-Americans use it frequently. It means "ass." Surprisingly, it's a rather vulgar word for something used so casually among children and elderly alike.

The other word that really sets the three waves apart is "Gacies." [It's pronounced Got-cheeses] Gacies means underwear. It's no longer used in modern Poland. It would be like saying "Bloomers" in English – no one says that anymore.

But we second-wave Polish-Americans, we use it. We use it just as much as "underwear."

When my mother was growing up, her grandmother was describing some people, perhaps on the news, that she deemed crazy. She said, "Those people are crazy! They must put gacies on sticks!"

It must have been the most bizarre thing my great-grandmother could think of to describe insane behavior. This saying was imprinted on my young mother, and she passed the phrase, "Crazy people with gacies on sticks!" on to me. Now I say it too.

Whenever I talk to another second-wave Polish-American and I use that phrase, even though it was clearly something my great-grandmother came up with herself. The funny thing is, they all agree. It makes sense that crazy people would put gacies on a stick. Because they're crazy!

Number 49: Free Entertainment

Time Length: 90 seconds

Categories/ Theme: Humorous, Slice of Life, Workplace, Relationships, Overhearing

Scene: A new employee talks to the HR Director about the coworker in the next cubicle

Thank you, Miss Jannet. Yes, my first week went really well. Everyone has been very nice to me.

The guy in the cubicle next to me? Oh, yeah. He's on the phone all the time—lots of personal calls. But it doesn't bother me; in fact, I find it hilarious!

It sounded like he was talking to his wife. He picked up the phone and said, 'Nomi?' I couldn't hear her side of the conversation, just some high-pitched noises. Suddenly, he says, 'No, I'm not having dinner.' You could almost feel her frustration through the phone!

He grumbled, 'Do whatever you want.'
Nomi must have really upset him because he sighed heavily before saying, 'Then throw it in the garbage then!'

I had to bite my lip to keep from laughing. I didn't want him to know I was eavesdropping!

It seemed like Nomi hung up after that because he called her back saying, 'Nomi, Nomi listen.' But she just yelled at him again!

He kept repeating her name like it was some sort of mantra—'Nomi, Nomi...' Then he sighed again and said, 'Nomi, I don't know why you got upset. I never eat dinner after work.'

I don't think he ever really apologized, but eventually, she calmed down because I didn't hear her yelling anymore. Then he wrapped up with a quick 'Goodbye,' probably rushing off to a meeting or something.

I guess I shouldn't have listened in so much, but it was hard not to—it was too funny! Honestly, it made for good background noise while I worked.

Oh! I hope my manager was pleased with my work so far?

He was? Great! Well, thank you for the feedback, Miss Jannet. Have a good day!

Number 50: No Jury Duty For Me Please

Time Length: 90 seconds

Categories/ Theme: Humorous, Situational, Law, Justice System, Satire

Scene: A potential Juror does not want to do Jury duty. S/he is standing in front of the group, reading off the whiteboard.

Juror number 32. My name is Rowan Smith. Occupation, stare at a screen all day hating my life... Also known as Admin slash working in an office. Spouse's occupation, veterinarian. Or my spouse could be one if you know one who's single. Oh! Sorry, your honor. I'll be more brief.

Education, pointless. I mean, Bachelor's in Science. Source of news, memes of course. татTV shows that I like. Have you seen the latest Off the Charts episode? I mean, who would have thought that Maggie would have– Oh, right! Off topic. Other TV shows include– Oh! That's enough? Okay cool.

Alright, hobbies. Well, I have a thing for collecting cameras. No, I'm not a photographer. I collect security cameras. All of them are operational. You want to see? I can view them on my phone!

I also like taking locks apart. I just lock a door and see if I can get out. I normally do. Alright, I had to jump out my window a couple times when I couldn't get out. That's what this scar on my elbow is from.

I also enjoy taking my car off-roading so I can practice driving really, really fast. I bet I could out-drive the co... I mean, not that I would ever need to. What? I have a clean record. Chill...

Okay, speaking of my car, I do not have any bumper stickers. I'm heavily against that. But if someone were to happen to put one on my car, it might be a little yellow electric mouse. You know, from that popular game or children's cartoon? But that's just hypothetical, of course.

Last question, have I ever served in the military? I don't think that would be a good idea... Oh, I'm dismissed? Oh, no... Well, have a good day, your honor. And good luck on your trial!

Number 51: I Can't Get Sick!

Time Length: 90 seconds

Categories/ Theme: Humorous, Anxiety, Situational, Workplace, Ambition

Scene: A worker has a big opportunity coming up and has a ton of anxiety leading up to it.

Next week is the big day! It won't be long now. I'm so nervous. It's okay. As long as I don't stress, formulate a good game plan, and most importantly, stay healthy, everything is going to be okay.

This is my chance for a new career opportunity—a chance to finally break free from this dead-end job. If I get sick now, it would ruin everything!

Wait! Did that old man just cough? It's okay. It's just one cough. And there's a good cubicle wall between us. I'm sure he covered his mouth. He's not gonna get me si—

Oh my gosh! He coughed again! Ugh! And he hacked a loogie into the trash can. That germy old man is going to get me sick!

No, no. Calm down. He's had a cough plenty of times, and he hasn't given me his illness before. That's because I avoid him like the plague! If anyone in this godforsaken place ever got the plague, it would be him! He's so disgusting! He licks his fingers all day long—every time he sorts through paper, it's just bleh-bleh-bleh all over his fingers! Worst of all, I saw him come out of the restroom once, and he only washed with water—just water! No soap!

Why won't the coughing stop? I know one way it could stop. That germ factory old man is pretty frail. What if I put my hands around his neck and choked him out? The coughing would stop then!

No... That stupid old man won't go quietly. He'll probably spit on me! Stupid germy old man! Why don't you just stop licking your fingers?!

Gah! I can't take it anymore! The coughing is nonstop! I need to get out of this incubator of an office! I need a new job!

Number 52: This is My Micromanager

Time Length: 90 seconds

Categories/ Theme: Humorous, Slice of Life, Workplace, Frustration, Breaking Point

Scene: Worker comes home early and tells their dwelling mate about their boss.

Yeah, I'm home early today. I just couldn't take it anymore. I need a vacation or a new job or something.

It's my boss again. I just don't get what his problem is! You know I'm a hard worker, and he knows that too—so of course, he piles on the tasks.

But lately, every single one sounds exactly the same! We've got "Put Away," then there's a "Put Away Report," a "Put Away Dashboard Report," and even a "Slotting Put Away Report." Seriously, how many reports about Put Aways do we need? No wonder I get confused!

Ugh, and sometimes he'll stop needing a report and won't tell me! So I'm just making it for no reason! It's so frustrating! Sometimes I stop doing these reports to see what happens, and you know what? Nothing happens! Like it never existed!

You'd think any complaints about me would revolve around the reports I stopped doing, but no! He nitpicks my regular tasks—assignments we've never had issues with before! He even dictates my emails and everything!

I'm starting to get really annoyed! I'm about to take his picture, put it on a tiny doll, and place it by my desk. That way when he starts hounding me, I can point to it and say, "This is my micromanager, so you can take a break!"

Number 53: Retail Story: Headset Radio

Time Length: 90 seconds

Categories/ Theme: Humorous, Situational, Slice of Life, Customer Service, Workplace

Scene: Retail worker discusses a unique customer. When speaking like the customer, use a funky voice.

The customers that come into this awful place are absolutely crazy! Today, I had this lady come in and ask for a headset radio. So I showed her the two options, and she requested the cheaper one. I rang it up, and it was $25.

She glared at me and said, "I can't afford it."

I thought she'd just walk out, but instead, she held her ground and stared at me like I could do something about it. After a few awkward seconds of her glaring at me, I said, "Okay. What do you want to do?"

"Well, I need that headset radio," she said.

"Okay, $25, please."

"I can't afford it," she repeated.

"Okay, do you have a coupon?"

"No."

"Do you have an email where I could send you a coupon?"

"No." Then she showed me the cash in her pocket and said, "This is what I got."

"Looks like you need twelve more dollars," I said.

"I can't afford it," she repeated one last time, her glare boring into my soul.

Honestly, part of me felt a little pity for her. I could tell she really wanted this headset radio but clearly didn't have the means to buy it. But at the end of the day, I'm just a minimum wage employee. My dad is forcing me to work here... He doesn't care if it makes me miserable! I could be doing so much better in college, but he just wants me to make money.

I just hate this place and wish I never had to come back here!

Despite her intense stare, I finally said, "I can't help you."

And finally—thank goodness—she left!

Number 54: Toddler Talk

Time Length: 90 seconds

Categories/ Theme: Humorous, Thematic, Family, Childhood, Misunderstanding

Scene: A relative reflects on a word that her niece continued to say as a toddler

Fee-jecht... Fee-jecht... What is Fee-jecht?

One time, I babysat my niece when she was two years old, and it was the most tiring thing I've ever done! That kid had so much energy! They say to have kids when you're young, but I was 16, and one day wore me out enough.

She kept bringing up this place that she called Fee-jecht. She was so fascinated by it too. I could not for the life of me figure out what the heck it was. Fee-jecht.

Exhausted, I convinced her to go on a magic carpet ride, just so I could sit down... She loved the idea, so I spread out a nearby towel, and as soon as she jumped into my lap, I pulled the towel around and pretended we were flying to Japan.

I did not get to rest long because as soon as we arrived in imaginary Japan, my little niece wanted to fly the magic carpet again. So I said, "How about England?" I pulled on the towel again and made whooshing sounds—ta-da, England!

She, of course, wanted to keep "flying," but before I could pick another place, my niece exclaimed, "Let's go to Fee-jecht!"

That word again! I had no idea what Fee-jecht was, but she really wanted to go there. She even gave me directions and soon we arrived in—you guessed it—Fee-jecht.

Fee-jecht... Fee-jecht... Fiji? What the heck is Fee-jecht?

(Gasp)

EGYPT! It's taken me more than 15 years, but I finally know what Fee-jecht is! Egypt! Of course! She must have seen the pyramids on TV. What kid wouldn't be fascinated by Egypt?

And you know what? I bet she hasn't thought of this at all since that day...

Number 55: The Chilling Churner

Time Length: 90 seconds

Categories/ Theme: Humorous, Horror, Thematic, Childhood, Supernatural, Satire

Scene: Neighbors discuss an urban legend.

You look tired. Something keeping you up at night, neighbor? The ice cream man? What, are you dating him or som– wait, which ice cream man? What time are you hearing the music exactly? You haven't checked the time? It wouldn't be at 3:13 AM, would it?

Oh no... This isn't good. I was wondering about all the recent disappearances. Now I understand. He's back...

The Chilling Churner! Legend says he appears when ice cream sales are down for five years straight. With the recent pandemic, people weren't buying much ice cream from trucks! Without sales, local ice cream workers can't pay to satisfy the ice cream maker! So he turns into the Chilling Churner and rides around at night. He lures unsuspecting children to his truck while their parents sleep. They say the children he targets are preplanned.

Sleep-deprived and naive, they sneak out for a late-night sweet treat. The Chilling Churner opens his back door, and the hypnotized child obediently walks inside. They say when the child enters, they're enveloped in white light. Slowly disappearing as the music plays and the doors close. Never to be seen again.

Then the Chilling Churner drives off. Blaring his music as if celebrating a victory.

I'm telling you! It's true! The Chilling Churner is real! I've seen him! His skin is all green and patchy! He's mostly bald but has a few strands poking out from under his cap! He's missing multiple teeth! And the whites of his eyes... they glow like the back of his truck!

I'm telling you, I've seen him! My parents stopped me before I went inside! I was four years old at the time! The police were called and everything! They never found him! He's been gone all this time... and now he's back.

Number 56: Eyes and Ears Open

Time Length: 90 seconds

Categories/ Theme: Humorous, Dramatic, Relationships, Emotional, Family, Anxiety

Scene: A parent encounters something he deems unsafe and then overly lectures his adult daughter on safety.

Excuse me. Excuse me, Miss. Excuse me!

Ugh! She can't hear me because she has her headphones in.

Hello! Sorry, I didn't mean to scare you. We are just in a hurry and wanted to get by you. Thank you.

(Turn to your daughter)

You see that? That's very dangerous! I could have been anyone and she would have absolutely no idea that I was coming! That's how young ladies get killed! Eyes and ears open! What do I always tell you? Eyes and ears open!

You never do that right? Not really? Not really! You never do that! You understand! You never ever do that! It doesn't matter if you were on your college campus, bad people are everywhere! Someone could come up behind you and hit you in the back of the head! You'd get knocked out and have no idea it was coming! They could knock you out, steal your phone, wallet, and you would have no idea what hit you all because you were listening to music! That's a dumb way to get killed!

Well, if they knock you out, they could do anything to you! You gotta be alert at all times! That's why you need to get rid of all unnecessary distractions!

And you never walk by yourself either! That makes you an easy target. If you see someone walking your way, cross the street! It doesn't matter if they look harmless. You don't know what's on their mind! Just cross the street!

You're not taking this seriously! It's a dangerous world out there! You just don't understand! You just float through life thinking nothing is gonna happen! You have to be prepared!

Well then, I hope you never have to learn this the hard way. Uh-huh. Yeah, I'll write that on your tombstone.

Number 57: You Have a Cat, Right?

Time Length: 90 seconds

Categories/ Theme: Humorous, Dramatic, Workplace, Conflict, Manipulation

Scene: A terrible boss who has a bad habit is trying to justify it by manipulating her employee.

Side note: Please, please don't lick your fingers if you do not intend to wash your hands shortly afterward or intend to touch surfaces being used by other people. The author absolutely hates this...

So, Robin, you have a cat, right?

(Pause)

Well, your cat is always licking himself. Doesn't that bother you?

(Pause)

Then how come you can't handle me licking my fingers whenever I turn pages? It seems very hypocritical of you. I don't understand what the difference is.

You see, you made me feel disgusting for licking my fingers. But the problem is, I have a condition where my skin doesn't produce enough oil to grip paper when I'm turning pages. And I can't use hand sanitizer in between thumbing through paperwork and using the computer. I have far too much work to do to be worrying about that.

I understand that you say you are a germaphobe, but I think you need to work on that issue. Everyone licks their fingers. Germs are just all around us; you just need to get used to it.

You really don't see my point?

Well, I brought up your cat because he probably licks himself all the time, and you have no problem petting him.

He doesn't leave the house... so that's why it's okay? You say he's basically quarantined, so he can't transfer germs to you? He still licks his ass all the time! But whatever. If you still feel like you need to wear gloves, kiddo, have at it.

Number 58: F*ck Friday

Time Length: 90 seconds

Categories/ Theme: Introspective, Dramatic, Social Commentary, Workplace, Frustration

Scene: A worker is no longer happy at the workplace and is evaluating society.

Happy Friday? Yeah... Happy...Friday... We all live for Friday... Our whole purpose in life is Friday.

We leave our comfortable homes that we love, where the thermostat is set just right, the furniture is comfortable, and we can wear whatever we want. No shoes! We leave our children, our spouses, our pets—all the people that we love. And for what?

A paycheck? A paycheck makes everything okay? A paycheck makes it worth putting on uncomfortable shoes, itchy clothes, sitting in a backbreaking chair in a freezing office full of people we have to act "professional" with?

For most of our week we pretend to be something that we're not. We care about something that doesn't matter to any of us. Our whole day is full of reports, spreadsheets and deadlines...

What are we even doing as a society? What is the point of this? There is no point... We're all just cogs in the machine. What the machine does, we don't know... We don't need to know...

All we care about is Friday... I hate Friday... Just another reminder that my life is ticking away and I'm not living it. I live to work, but all I want is to work to live... I don't think it's that hard to ask...

Number 59: Overwhelmed

Time Length: 90 seconds

Categories/ Theme: Introspective, Thematic, Anxiety, Psychological, Thoughtful

Scene: Patient talks to a therapist

Thank you for agreeing to squeeze me in on such short notice Dr. Winecough. I hope you are doing well. How are the kids? Oh! Yes... I'm stalling. Right.

Well, I'm actually feeling pretty good. I can't say I'm unhappy, but I can't say I'm exactly content with my life either. I guess the best way to describe how I'm feeling is... overwhelmed. I have a lot of decisions to make right now.

As you know, I hate my job, but where do I go next? I no longer want to be in Admin anymore, but what else can I actually do? We both know what I want to do, but can I actually succeed in it? We know how it went the last time I tried something similar in the arts... I ended up in Admin... A published author, but I certainly don't feel like one whenever I'm sitting at my desk for hours a day. Forced to sit there quietly, the whole time, five days a week. I just don't want to do that anymore.

So what am I doing to get out of this situation? Nothing... I've made zero progress since we last saw each other. I just can't decide when and where to go next, even if I know what I want to do next.

On top of that, I desperately need a new vehicle... Of course, with the current state of the economy, everything is much more expensive than it was only a couple years ago. So I need to make sure that I choose the right vehicle, but again, which one? On one hand, I love how my current car is small and fuel efficient, but I can't help but imagine what it would be like to have a much bigger vehicle. Like a camper van so I could live in that for a while. Just so I could escape my current situation.

What do you say, Dr. Winecough? What should I do?

Number 60: How Did This Happen?

Time Length: 90 seconds

Categories/ Theme: Introspective, Political, Social Commentary, Informative, Ethics, Morality

Scene: This is coming from a very frustrated voter who still loves the country that she lives in.

It's election year again... Who am I going to vote for? Ugh... Does it even really matter at this point?

Even though multiple people run for office, only two of them have a chance to win. And because only one of the two main parties can win, everyone abandons their own morals, wants, and needs in hopes of preventing the party they don't like from winning. This creates a political climate where the government, which is supposed to represent the majority of citizens, doesn't actually represent 95% of them!

Instead, it represents two extremes that are both equally manipulative, illogical, immoral, and uncompromising. This is a huge problem for a political system designed to create and enforce laws by compromising with opposing views to create the best law for the majority of people. But everyone is running on fear of their rights being taken away.

Meanwhile, these sleazy politicians take our rights away, fill their own pockets using their knowledge of the law, news, and stock market, and hide amongst the good ones who are actually trying to help the country.

How did we even get here? How is it that politicians who would actually listen to the American people get ousted by the parties they align with?

I still feel like the best presidential candidate who could have made a difference was completely destroyed by her own party. I look at the candidates on the podium now and get so angry that she is not standing there. She was the bridge between the two parties, but the two parties want to keep fighting with each other so they can continue to keep this toxic system in place.

So who will I vote for? Red or Blue? I literally don't want to vote for either, and neither should you! If we want real change, we need to vote for someone else.

Number 61: Lasting Pain

Time Length: 90 seconds

Categories/ Theme: Introspective, Dramatic, Medical, Health, Frustration

Scene: A injured person explains her frustrations over a leg injury

Every morning, I wake up with aching in my knee. Some days it's worse than others, but I can never predict what I'm going to get.

On very bad days, not only does my knee hurt, but my hip and ankle do too. My hip is always cracking. Even if I rest my leg all day or do the exercises that the doctor gave me, nothing seems to help.

There are times when I think it's going to get better! That I'm finally going to put this injury behind me—but then the pain comes back.

I miss jogging. I never thought I'd ever say that, but I do. I miss being active. I miss dancing. Most of all, I miss walking at a fast pace and being able to walk for miles without worrying about pain. I'm sick of being in pain.

I come from a family of fast walkers, and my boss has a quick pace too. I can't keep up with any of them anymore. People don't notice because I can stand and walk, but I have to be very careful. I have to watch each step, or I might set off the pain again.

I don't know what to do. Why won't it heal? Do I need surgery? Do I need injections? What am I going to do? What if the recovery time is long, and I have to hold off on everything that I've planned for next year? I just wish I knew what was wrong—and more than that, how to make it stop. Why won't the pain just stop?

What am I going to do...?

Number 62: A Complex Case

Time Length: 90 seconds

Categories/ Theme: Introspective, Dramatic, Law, Justice System, Morality

Scene: A defense attorney sees the victim mocking his client after the sentencing hearing.

Look at them laughing. They think this is a joke. My client's going to spend three years in jail, and they find it funny.

I know my client was guilty of hurting that girl over there, but somehow I don't feel good about him going to prison. At least we managed to reduce his sentence from six years to three.

I understand she's the victim, and her friends are here to support her, but I can't help feeling like I'm back in high school, watching the "weird kid" get sent to the principal's office.

He's not a bad guy. He made a mistake. He's been in jail for months and knows what he did was wrong. But this isn't an evil man; this is a deeply troubled individual—someone who's battled addiction and depression, who lost his brother young.

He was in pain, and the evidence shows the "victim" pushed him to his breaking point. She accused him of cheating publicly on social media. He tried to stay quiet, but one day, he couldn't hold back. He hit her repeatedly, trying to silence her accusations. He didn't want to kill her; he just wanted her to stop.

Why didn't he leave? They had a kid, and he already had another baby momma trying to take custody of his other child. That's her over there, laughing the loudest. Don't think she's great though; her other child was just taken away for child abuse accusations.

I want to feel bad for the victim. I want it to be simple: he hit her, he's bad, end of story. But their laughter doesn't sit right with me.

What a messed up world. Hard to see who the real devils are, or who belongs behind bars.

Number 63: Do I Really Have to Date?

Time Length: 90 seconds

Categories/ Theme: Introspective, Frustration, Thematic, Empowerment, Social Commentary

Scene: An artist discusses her stress of societal expectations versus her desires to create.

I know everyone's just trying to help, but honestly? It's hurting my feelings. Why is it that whenever I start raving about all the amazing projects I'm working on, people immediately ask about my dating life? As if all these things I'm doing are just... overcompensating for loneliness. That's not the case at all!

Even when I was in a relationship, I spent so much time wishing I was creating something new rather than being with him. It made me feel guilty, like I was a bad person for prioritizing my artwork and creative projects over my partner. I've told people about this, and they just say I didn't love him enough. But if that's true, how is any random guy off the street supposed to be different?

(Pause, softer tone)
I was happier when I truly didn't want a romantic partner anymore. I was finally at peace with being single. But when so many people bombard you with questions about dating, you start asking those questions yourself. Then you start feeling like there's something wrong with you for not dating. And then... you start to feel empty.

(Hesitates, then continues with a mix of hope and resignation)

The truth is, I think I've found the one I want. He just isn't... available at the moment. If I complete my projects, maybe he'll notice me!

(Sighs)
But... we all know that likely won't happen. My other projects didn't go anywhere after all. How will this time be any different?

(Bitter laugh)
Right. It won't. And everyone knows that, so...

(Pause, then with forced enthusiasm)
I guess the only thing to do is to start dating. Yay...

(Final pause, then quietly)
But is that really what I want? Or just what everyone else wants for me?

Number 64: What Else Do You Want to Do?

Time Length: 90 seconds

Categories/ Theme: Introspective, Inspirational, Thematic, Self-Discovery, Empowerment

Scene: A person makes a positive revelation about a question that used to bother her in childhood

When I was a kid, many adults in my life would ask me, "What do you want to be when you grow up?" or "What are your career prospects?" I would answer that I wanted to be an artist, a writer. But many of these adults—though not all—would give me a fake smile and say, "Oh, cool. What else do you want to do?"

That always bothered me; it felt like they didn't believe in my abilities. And then I wouldn't believe in them either. I heard that many artists received that same question, and they felt the same way.

As an adult, I realized that this question can actually be a good one. It shouldn't just be asked of artists—writers, performers, dancers, designers—but also of the practical kids.

You want to be a doctor? That's great! What else do you want to do? You want to be a police officer? That's cool! What else? You want to work for the government? Awesome! What else?

We should be asking this question every day—not in a dismissive way the adults asked me as a child, but with genuine encouragement. The subtext should feel like a pat on the back: "Amazing job at your one career. Now... what else do you want to do?"

We live in a world where we are more connected than anyone in history ever was. We can communicate, sell, distribute, and travel faster than ever before! We can solve problems for even the littlest things—like doing the dishes—we can use a dishwasher. Want to spend less time cooking? Try an affordable meal service! Don't like commuting? Work from home!

So why are we still asking children, "What do you want to be when you grow up?" Instead, we should be asking, "What are ALL the things you want to be and do when you grow up?" You can do it all! Just try—and keep trying every day. What else do you want to do?

Number 65: A Case in the Night Owl's Favor

Time Length: 90 seconds

Categories/ Theme: Introspective, Informative, Humorous, Empowerment, Social Commentary

Scene: A night owl was teased for sleeping in. This conversation leads to a bit of teasing back and defending later chronotypes.

You go to bed at 9:30? That's the middle of the day! And you get up at 5 AM? Seriously? In the middle of the night? It's still dark then!

Look, I don't need to change my sleep schedule. I just have a different chronotype. In fact, the whole 'early bird gets the worm' thing is a modern construct. Humans naturally have different sleep patterns. It's an evolutionary trait that helped us survive in ancient times.

Think about it: Ancient humans lived in nomadic tribes. There were no modern homes to keep them safe from wildlife at night. No gas or electric heating that stayed running with the push of a button.

Someone had to stay on the lookout for predators or rival tribes looking to steal resources. Someone had to keep the fire alive all night long while the others slept.

That's who I would have been during ancient times – the lookout and fire keeper! The tribes needed the night owls just as much as the early risers.

So no, I don't think I need to conform to society. Instead, we as a society should be more empathetic to the sleep cycle needs of others. We should stop pretending that we all can and want to live identical lives.

Yes, I know I sound like a hypocrite for teasing you about your early morning routines, but that's what I was doing – teasing. My point still stands: I'm a night owl, and there's nothing wrong with that.

Number 66: What People Say Is About Them, But Should I Hear About Me?

Time Length: 90 seconds

Categories/ Theme: Introspective, Inspirational, Relationships, Social Commentary, Empowerment

Scene: The speaker reacts to how her creative goals are sometimes taken by other people based on their perspective.

What people say is about them; what you hear is about you. When my friends steer conversations about my creative goals toward dating, I've realized they're really saying, "Being in a relationship makes me happy, and I want that for you too." But what I used to hear was something entirely different - a criticism of my life, suggesting my creative pursuits were just an overcompensation for being single.

My last relationship taught me that finding life's meaning solely in a relationship isn't healthy. It's unfair to expect a partner to be your sole source of happiness. If you're not content with yourself, no amount of effort from your partner can fix that. My ex made me feel like a show poodle he'd grown bored of. No matter how hard I tried to please him, it never met his unrealistic standards. My creative goals grounded me—they reminded me of what I truly wanted in life. I realized someone like him wasn't what I wanted.

So far, a life where my creative goals–whatever crazy idea that I come up with next–as the center of my universe, makes me happy.

I don't need to stop being creative and focus on finding a relationship because what people say is about them; what I hear is about me. Now that I heard it, I will choose what I actually hear. And what I hear now is, "You're so amazing, how are you still single?" And that is a compliment!

Number 67: What Happened?

Time Length: 90 seconds

Categories/ Theme: Introspective, Dramatic, Art, Self-Discovery, Anxiety

Scene: An artist voices her struggles of creating a piece.

What happened? Why have I slowed down? I was so passionate about this task before me. I was working on it every day.

But now, I've slowed down. Why? Why do I do this? What am I afraid of? The end? I shouldn't be. The ending is just a new beginning.

Yes, I know that. Logically, I understand. Procrastinating on finishing this project isn't going to make it last longer. It won't preserve the joy it's brought me. I can always start again. I can always create something new. But I can't move on to another project without finishing this one. There is no second without the first.

I get it, but I can't help how I feel. I want this masterpiece to last forever. I want it to be perfect. I don't want to put it out too soon and regret it later.
I need to finish it! There's so much life this project wants to give to the world. It has so much potential once it's completed. I can't hold it back from what it's meant to be—the people it's meant to influence and the plans I have for it.

No... I must accept it and believe in it. It's good, really good—great even. I can't hoard it like a dragon in a lair full of treasure. I will finish it. I'm ready to finish it. Just one last piece and... it is done.

Number 68: Elizabeth Tower and Big Ben

Time Length: 90 seconds

Categories/ Theme: Wistful, Travel, Descriptive, Cultural, Self-Discovery

Scene: A traveler is mesmerized by seeing Elizabeth Tower and Big Ben for the first time.

I made sure to see Big Ben while I was in London. Well, Big Ben and Elizabeth Tower. Big Ben is actually just the clock part.

Seeing it for the first time was surreal. I had already visited the Tower of London and other local monuments, but nothing compared to standing before Big Ben. I've seen it countless times in movies, pictures, and video games, but experiencing it in real life was entirely different.

I couldn't believe how easy it was to find. I expected to arrive at the nearest subway station and have a bit of a walk, but no…

Right when I left the underground, BAM! There it was! It loomed over me, gazing down as if studying me. Looking at the yellow glow of the clock, I felt like I had traveled through time, witnessing everything it had seen over its 160 years. In that moment, I became part of its amazing history.

I was among all the incredible people—past, present, and future—who had stood in its gaze, examined by a structure that felt all-knowing.

It had a soul...and I felt it. It was...beautiful. Though I didn't stare for long, every second felt like a gift. My heart changed after seeing that building. I felt like I was now smarter, stronger, braver, and more mature—like England itself had accepted me.

I relive this moment whenever I look at the pictures I took. What a magnificent piece of architecture! Not frozen in time but thriving as the days go by.

Number 69: Why the Love Potion Didn't Work

Time Length: 90 seconds

Categories/ Theme: Wistful, Romance, Dramatic, Fantasy, Misunderstanding, Love

Scene: A young witch gave a potion to her crush, but it didn't work. The side effect of it not working is death in three years.

I'm so sorry, Casey. I've been avoiding you because I've made a terrible mistake. You see, I'm a witch, and I'm very skilled with potions. I slipped one into the muffins I made you—the really tasty ones you said you didn't want to share with anyone.

The potion I gave you was a love potion. It's true. I have feelings for you. I really, really like you. I might actually love you. We are great friends, and I wanted more than that. So, I thought if I gave you the potion, you would ask me out, and we could officially be a couple.

But nothing changed after I gave it to you. You didn't treat me any differently; you looked at me the same way as before. You never made the move to ask me out.

I checked to see if perhaps I made the potion wrong, but I followed each step exactly as written in the spell book. I'm normally a natural when it comes to brewing potions, so I'm almost positive that I made it correctly.

Then I looked up what it means if the potion doesn't work, and it said you're going to die in three years! I'm so, so sorry! That's why I couldn't face you! I just couldn't bear it! I—I killed you... In three years, you're going to die all because I was selfish and wanted to love you more than you loved me!

(She cries)

What? What are you saying? Y—You mean—the reason it didn't work was that you—like me back? R—really?

Oh Casey! I can't believe it! You truly like me? You want to be my boyfriend? I'm so happy! So that means the potion didn't work because you already loved me! That means you're going to be okay! Come on! Let's tell everyone the great news!

Number 70: Daisy Award

Time Length: 90 seconds

Categories/ Theme: Wistful, Medical, Dramatic, Emotional, Health

Scene: A nurse assists an emergency room patient who has a severe phobia of needles. The nurse shows incredible empathy, compassion and skill while serving the patient.

Leighton, this way please. Let's get you a wheelchair.

So, what brings you in tonight? Abdominal pain on the right side? Alright, we'll get you some pain medicine soon. Are those tears from the pain, or... Ah, I see. You're afraid of needles. A severe phobia? Just the initial stick bothers you, but once it's in, you're okay? Good to know.

Listen, Leighton, I understand you're in a lot of pain right now. I want to help you as quickly as possible, but to do that, we need to start an IV and run some tests. It's perfectly okay to be scared. But I promise you, I'm excellent at placing IVs. I'll do it so fast, you'll barely notice. You can trust me on this.

Can you look me in the eyes for a moment? I give you my word - I'm skilled at this. I'll make sure to do it perfectly so you don't have to be afraid. You won't pass out, I promise. I'm here to take care of you.

Would you prefer a countdown, or should I just do it? Alright, I'll just go ahead and... there, all done. See? I told you I was good. Now, we'll give you some pain medication to make you more comfortable. After that, the technicians will come in for a

CT scan. The doctor will review the results and explain what's going on.

You're welcome, Leighton. I hope you feel better soon.

Number 71: My Kitten's Rescue

Time Length: 90 seconds

Categories/ Theme: Wistful, Slice of Life, Animal/Nature, Overcoming Adversity, Descriptive

Scene: A person was just caught daydreaming about her pet. Then describes how the pet almost died.

Oh! I was just thinking about Riley when he was a kitten. He was so little! I can't believe I was able to pick him up with one hand. He was just a ball of fluff, weighed no more than a feather.

Now look at him. He looks exactly the same, just bigger. I can't lift him the way that I used to, but he's still that same little ball of fluff he always was.

I'm so thankful that he got to grow up. Did you know he was injured when he arrived? Oh, yes. He must have narrowly missed a bird of prey or something. Because of his black fur and the fact that he wasn't actively bleeding, we didn't see the wounds.

But he started to slow down and couldn't jump anymore. It was very odd for such a young kitten—kittens are supposed to be full of energy and playing all the time—but Riley just slept. Then he wasn't able to use his back legs anymore; he just dragged them wherever he went.

We took him to the vet, but she didn't see what was wrong with him. She assumed he had worms and dewormed him. It didn't work; he just got worse.

We got a second opinion, and that's when the wounds were found. This poor little kitten, only weeks old, was dying from an infection.

He was prescribed antibiotics, and within two days, he was able to stand up on his back legs again! Slowly, he took some shaky steps. Then later in the day, he wanted to play again!

I still have the video! I'll show you! My gosh! He was so little. Oh, I wish they could stay that way forever. But look at my beautiful boy now! I love him so much! Thank God he healed up!

Number 72: I Just Love to Talk

Time Length: 90 seconds

Categories/ Theme: Wistful, Dramatic, Inspirational, Self-Discovery, Ambition

Scene: A person discovers a career purpose later in life.

If I had known that being a voice actor was something I could do and make a living off of, I would have done it years ago. I love talking. I don't necessarily need to talk to someone, I just kind of like the act of talking. I'm always talking to myself. I once even talked so much as a child that I gave myself laryngitis.

I thought it was a flaw at the time and from thereon after too. I tried to force myself to be quieter, to be polite and behave. But maybe I found a career where I don't have to do that. Where I can just talk and talk for hours and no one tells me to shut up. If they don't want to hear my voice, well they can just shut it off.

I don't need anyone to listen to me. I just want to express myself, freely, emotionally. Not keep it all bottled up inside all day. Not having to be perfect and professional, but angry or happy or sad or whatever other emotions I could bring a voice to. This could really be the answer to all my problems. My finances, my mental health, my social life, everything! I've been told I have a great voice - my old boss at the doctor's office thought so. She said I sound great on the phone!

I always thought voice acting was all about doing impressions. Ugh, whenever I try to do an impression, it always comes out flat and sounding the same. But I found out that you don't need to be able to change your voice and do impressions to be a voice actor. That's only one type of voice acting. There are commercials, and all kinds of stuff out there! I found this course online where I can learn more about it!

So I'm gonna do it! I'm going to be a voice actor!

Number 73: Not a Good Husband

Time Length: 90 seconds

Categories/ Theme: Wistful, Humorous, Relationships, Animal/ Nature, Slice of Life

Scene: A woman discusses how her late husband treated her on their honeymoon.

Thank you for your condolences, but my late husband was not a good husband. In fact, on our honeymoon, we went camping in the woods and were warned by the park ranger that bears were in the area. He instructed that we must store all food in our cars before we go to bed just in case a bear wanders by our cabin.

That night, my husband and I celebrated our nuptials with various types of liquor given to us as wedding gifts. One of them happened to be mead. The alcohol made me very sleepy so I ended up turning in earlier than usual and left my husband the duty of securing our food and drinks in the car.

Well, I woke up in the middle of the night and saw that not only did my husband not put the food away, but he left the half-empty bottle of mead open on the kitchen table. Do you know what mead is made out of? Honey! Do you know what bears like? Honey!

So I woke my husband and scolded him for not putting the mead away. He grumbled that I was paranoid and left me with the task to gather all the leftovers and put them in the car, alone, at night.

But now, looking back, I think I know why he was not concerned about the bears like I was. You see, we did not carry any weapons with us since we were from out of the country. So if a bear did come to attack us, I think his plan was to feed me to the bears. He'd feed me to the bears and he would run away.

But everything would be okay... for him. And that's all that ever mattered... to him. From our very first day as husband and wife, to his very last day, it was always about him.

Number 74: You Did Your Best

Time Length: 90 seconds

Categories/ Theme: Wistful, Law, Mentorship, Justice System, Self-Discovery

Scene: A mentor consoles a young defense attorney after he loses his first case.

Look, kid, it happens. You win some and you lose some. It's all part of the job.

You care a lot right now. Understandable. You put a lot of time and energy into making a good case for the client. You believed he was innocent and you made a great case towards that verdict. But listen, sometimes the evidence is just too damming. Sometimes, the prosecution has a smoking gun in the hand of your client, and there's nothing you can do about it.

At the end of the day, we have a job to do. We need to represent our side to the best of our ability with the information that we have. Sure, we became lawyers for the salary, but we had to work hard to get to where we are. We all studied law because we love the law. Deep down, we believe in the justice system that we live under.

Remember, the guilty have the same right to an attorney as the innocent. You might be a great lawyer if all your clients won their cases, but you still want to be a good person. You don't want to win for the sake of winning. You want the case done right. Sometimes, you find yourself on the wrong side.

You did great out there. You should be proud. I'm proud of you.

Don't worry. It gets easier. In about six to eight years or so, you'll have seen everything and become jaded like the rest of us.

You're in a great place right now. It's not gonna last forever. You care deeply. Learn from it, enjoy it, and remember that tomorrow you'll start your next case.

Number 75: Vincent's Muse

Time Length: 90 seconds

Categories/ Theme: Wistful, Dramatic, Historical Fiction, Art, Fantasy

Scene: A muse tells a story of a time she inspired Vincent van Gogh to paint. Note that a different painting could be subbed to make this monologue fit the performer.

A muse's job never ends. We inspire artists when they hit creative blocks. One night, I entered a painter's studio in Belgium. The air was thick with turpentine and linseed oil. In the center, hunched over and sniffling, sat Vincent.

I whispered, "How about giving it another go? Start with a color. Any color." Vincent wiped his eyes and began covering a canvas with various hues of green.

When he paused, I suggested, "Now, think of what inspires you. Paint what you love."

He grabbed another brush, and for a moment, I felt his gaze lock onto me. Impossible, I thought. We muses are invisible to humans. Yet, as he painted, that feeling persisted.

As an image emerged, a chill ran through me. The woman's features were impossibly familiar.

Vincent stepped back. "Done," he said simply.

I looked, transfixed. How could I not? Seeing completed works is a muse's greatest perk after all. But this... the woman Vincent had painted was me.

"Portrait of Woman in Blue," Vincent murmured, his eyes meeting mine with startling clarity. "I thank you."

That's when I knew this man was different. A true master artist who could sense creativity itself, as if he could see it with his own eyes.

It was one of the most fulfilling moments of my time as a muse—an experience I've chased ever since.

Number 76: The Persian Messenger

Time Length: 90 seconds

Categories/ Theme: Wistful, Renaissance Faire, Romance, Cultural, Historical Fiction, Love

Scene: The local Innkeeper is looking for a message from a former guest. This is the story behind why.

Any messages for the Inn? Any for the Innkeeper? Perhaps my daughter? Oh, she will be so disappointed... We thought surely he would have written by now.

A few months ago, we had unusual visitors—a caravan of five men from Persia. They claimed to be on their way to send a message to the Queen, though we are miles from the capital. One joked that perhaps fairies made them veer off their path.

It was dark when they arrived, so I told them, 'I am the town's Innkeeper. If thou art not needing to leave for London immediately, thou art welcome to stay here for the night.' They graciously accepted and paid handsomely. I never knew foreigners could be so pleasant.

While they visited, my daughter, bless her, had a night where she could not sleep. One of the Persian messengers was awake as well, and they spent the evening telling stories. He shared tales of his travels, and my daughter, who loves to tell tales herself, shared some of her best stories with him. I managed to save some coin for her education, so she is quite skilled at telling interesting tales.

She told me that he became a messenger because he loved learning and hearing stories. An interest they both seemed to share. The messengers stayed for five days. Each evening, my daughter and the young man exchanged tale after tale.

When it was time for them to leave, the young man promised my daughter he would send word and return soon. I always expected her to take over the Inn, but seeing her with that Persian messenger, I think I know where her heart belongs.

So if thou get any word from a man from Persia, please come to me right away.

Number 77: You Never Disappoint Me, Darling

Time Length: 90 seconds

Categories/ Theme: Wistful, Romance, Introspective, Love, Emotional

Scene: A woman describes why she loves a man as if she's talking to him.

You are the first and only man I've ever truly wanted. It's hard for me to put my feelings for you into words because I love everything about you—your flaws, your gentleness, your handsomeness, your talent, your voice, and how you react to things. I've never loved anyone like this before. Normally, when I find a flaw in a man, my interest fades, but with you, my love only grows stronger.

I even love the individual hairs on your face. All I want to do is caress you, run my fingers through your raven hair, and kiss you. At the same time, I want to sit with you, learn more about you, and learn from you. I love watching your eyes sparkle whenever you talk about your passions. You say you're not a smart man, but I disagree; you're much wiser than you think. You're trying to be humble, but everyone who meets you can see how kind you are. It's not just what you say but how you interact with the world that matters.

I've never seen a man with such strong arms touch things so gently. When you touched my shoulder for a picture, it felt like a butterfly landed on me—I was shocked!

I know I can be forceful and impatient at times, but you don't seem to struggle with that at all. You have complete control at all times, and I admire that about you; it's one of countless things that make you successful.

I want you to know that you're the most beautiful thing on this earth. You bring me so much joy and never disappoint me. I know you do your best every day—and none of it is for me—but regardless, I appreciate everything you've taught me.

I love you, Darling.

120-Second (2 minute) Monologues

Number 78: My Feelings of Love are not Crazy

Time Length: 120 seconds

Categories/ Theme: Dramatic, Introspective, Thematic, Love, Conflict

Scene: A person is incredibly offended about how her feelings for a performer are judged so she defends herself.

Stalker? Delusional? Mental health issue? Seriously? Why? Because I fell in love with a performer? Is that really that crazy? Is he somehow no longer a person because he performs on stage? Am I not able to become a performer because I'm currently not on stage?

Is it really that far-fetched that two people could vibe with each other? That an unworldly connection might exist between them? Not logical but purely emotional?

Is there truly no such thing as fate? No destiny? Should we say that God doesn't exist either because science can't definitively prove his existence?

What is love anyway? Am I supposed to just pick someone at random and just make it work? News flash! I tried that once! Allowed someone to dictate my whole future. Ignored my own needs just to keep him around... Why bother?

Why can't I have the performer anyway? What is so wrong with me that I can't have him? It's not like I just saw him on TV and decided he was the one. No! I feel an intense emotion wash over me whenever he's around. I swear I can sense him and pick him out of a crowd.

One time, my friend and I were walking the wrong direction to the theater. I kept insisting we needed to turn around. Sure enough, when we did, I led us straight there. And no, I've never been there before! I just know him by how he feels in my heart.

How does this make me a stalker or mentally ill? Could there really be a bond between us that can't be explained? Hasn't there been thousands of love stories literally dictating this kind of thing happening? What do people mean by, "Love is not like the movies and people need to stop looking for that?" Then what is it then? Can someone tell me?

No! Let me tell you! I have never felt like this around anyone else before in my entire life! There's something special here and I know it!

Okay fine! Maybe he's not the love of my life. Maybe he's supposed to guide me to where I'm supposed to go. Maybe he's supposed to be someone important in my life. If that makes me crazy for feeling that way then so be it!

Number 79: The Abandoned Gray

Time Length: 120 seconds

Categories/ Theme: Dramatic, Sci-fi, Relationships, Transformation, Friendship, Love

Scene: A person is confronted because he has taken the place of an alien. He turns out to actually be the alien.

No, don't be afraid. I'm sure you were looking for a tiny gray alien. He's still here, don't you worry. That little alien is me. I am Gray.

You see, my people used to abduct your people for experiments, but I was part of an organization that fought against it. I've always liked humans. It fascinates me how every single one of you looks so unique from each other. Even when your DNA is nearly identical, you still look and act different from one another.

It's the complete opposite from my people. All of us are the same size, color, and shape. We can barely tell the difference between male and female. Most of us think the same as well, which is why those of us that fought against the abductions were ostracized. My people believe that your people are violent, greedy, and murderers, but I believe they use that logic as an excuse for their abductions and experiments.

I destroyed the technology that the abductors used to kidnap your people. My team completely wiped out the information to build new ones. It will take them decades to rebuild and start their abduction experiments again. Without the blueprints, they can no longer create a stable beam to lift humans into the ship. They'll have to start from scratch.

For our crimes, we were abandoned on Earth. I'll never forget what they said as they dropped each of us in different parts of the world: "Now you will see how evil and unforgiving the humans truly are."

After being here for days, I began to think they were right, but then you came along. Melinda, you showed me what human kindness is. You gave me shelter and even gave me a name. Because of that, I transformed into a human. Now I'm just like you.

Will you allow me to stay by your side? Will you still accept me as a human, not just as a helpless alien? I know it's a lot to ask, but you've shown me a kindness I've never known before. Thank you, Melinda. I promise, I will forever repay your kindness.

Number 80: Truth or Dare

Time Length: 120 seconds

Categories/ Theme: Dramatic, Suspense, Manipulation, Revenge, Supernatural

Scene: Frenemies are on a beach. One gets the upper hand.

Hey guys! I found this bottle on the beach. Since we have nothing else to do, let's play Truth or Dare!

What? No, I'm not planning anything! You really don't think much of me, do you? It's just a game! Let's sit in a circle—Great! I'll go first!

Truth or Dare? (Points) Landed on you, Ash. Okay, I dare you to keep your arms crossed until I tell you to uncross them. Heh, now you have to spin that bottle without your hands! Haha!

Well, not a great spin with your feet, but it looks like it landed on me. I'll pick Truth. Why did I want to play this game? That's easy—I thought it would be fun.

Okay, my turn again. (Points) Landed on you, Ruth. Dare? I dare you to talk only if I address you; otherwise, you must remain mute.

Oh, looks like you can't talk now! You lose your turn, and I get to go again. No! It's plenty fair, Ash; calm down!

Now... (Points) Oh, lands on Ruth again. Truth or Dare? Truth? Perfect! Is it true that you purchased cocaine and placed it in my bag so that the policeman would find it and send me to jail?

(Pause to hear her answer.)

I knew it... You still can't talk unless I allow it, so you lose another turn! (Points) Lands on Ruth again. Truth or Dare?

No Ash! This game is just beginning! We stop when I say we stop!

Dare? I dare you to swim in the ocean until I tell you to stop.

What's the matter, Ash? Can't stand up without using your arms? That's the point.

You see this bottle had a message. It said that I have the power to play Truth or Dare and make it go my way. Once you all decided to play, you've been at my mercy. Now Ruth will continue swimming in the ocean until I command her to stop.

And you, Ash—with your arms crossed—you can't harm me. And Wendy? You better go get your friend if you don't want her to drown.

Had a great time playing with you all. See ya!

Number 81: What Do You Want to Do?

Time Length: 120 seconds

Categories/ Theme: Dramatic, Relationships, Frustration, Conflict, Abuse, Manipulation

Scene: A woman complains about her ex's sexual needs.

I enjoy painting—it's my favorite thing to do. If I could, I'd paint all day. But when I had a boyfriend, I knew that I needed to spend time with him too.

At first, it was fine. I painted some days and spent time with him on others. But over time, he started to require more of my attention. He expected my full focus whenever he was home and got agitated if I took out my brushes or set up my canvas.

I tried to compromise by asking him to model for me, but he always declined. He'd say he didn't feel like standing still or sitting for a portrait. He had let me paint him once when we first started dating, but that was ages ago. Now, he'd complain that he missed me and wanted to spend time together, so I'd put my canvas away and sit beside him.

After a while, he'd ask, "What do you want to do?"

This annoyed me because he knew exactly what I wanted—painting! Instead of saying that, I'd reply that I didn't know.

"You don't know?" he'd ask with those big blue eyes.

"I don't," I'd say.

"Oh. What to do?" That's when I realized he wanted one thing—the thing that he always wanted to do, which happened to be the one thing I didn't want to do.

Not wanting to hurt his feelings, I'd say, "Well, you didn't want to model for me."

He'd agree but try to look cute, which only irritated me more. He knew what he wanted but wanted it to be my idea.

Finally, I'd say, "If you can't figure something out, I'm going back to painting."

"Painting?" he'd ask, amused.

"Yes! That's what I wanted before!"

Then it would be his turn to say, "Oh, I don't know."

Did he think I was oblivious?

Sometimes I'd pretend not to understand his hints so I could get back to painting. For the rest of the day, he'd mope around and smoke weed until he passed out on the couch. Adorable, right?

Number 82: Saving a Child from a Predator

Time Length: 120 seconds

Categories/ Theme: Dramatic, Thematic, Situational, Emotional, Suspense, Overcoming Adversity

Scene: A bystander witnesses a potential child abduction and decides to act.

Hey! Did you just offer candy to a child?

Hi, Sweetie. Do you know this man? You don't? She said she doesn't know you! Why are you talking to this child? You weren't doing anything? Sure! I saw you standing there doing nothing!

Sweetie, cover your ears for a little bit.

Sir, I'm gonna have to ask you to leave! Back up! Get the hell away from this little girl right now! Oh, oh! You were just being nice? You were just trying to make friends? She doesn't need friends like you! You're too old! She said she doesn't know you! Back the hell up now! I will put my hands on you if you get any closer to us! I mean it! BACK THE HELL UP!

(Pause as he leaves)

He's leaving. Okay, you can uncover your ears now, Sweetheart. I need you to stay seated on the bench, okay? I need to make a quick phone call to the police so that weirdo doesn't come back.

Who are you here with today? Your mom? Where is she? Okay, stay right here. We'll wait for her together.

Hello? I need a police officer dispatched to the park. A strange man was here trying to lure a child with candy. Yes, I have a description. Old, gray hair but balding. He had on a dark gray hoodie and jeans. I think he was wearing name brand sneakers—really clean, nice looking, brand new—oh, hold on a minute. I think the little girl's mom just arrived.

Hi there. I'm on the phone with the police. A strange man just came up and tried to offer your baby candy. I stepped in, and he's gone now. You only turned around for a second? Yeah, kids will do that. I see you have three other ones with you. You definitely have your hands full. I can help you watch them until the police arrive.

(Back to the phone)

They said an officer will be here in five minutes. They may want to talk to your daughter when they get here. Did you see a man with balding gray hair and brand new sneakers walking around? No? You don't know anyone matching that description?

No, he didn't give a name. I didn't give him a chance to give one; I told him to leave right away!

You're welcome. I have kids too. I would hope someone would protect my children like this if they needed it. You're welcome!

Number 83: What Are You Doing in the Bushes?

Time Length: 120 seconds

Categories/ Theme: Dramatic, Suspense, Morality, Conflict, Psychological, Ethics

Scene: A stalker struggles with his moral compass

It's been three weeks now since I first saw her, and I can't seem to get enough. I never intended to follow her home, but somehow, I found myself doing it. Thankfully, her house has many bushes to hide in. I was only supposed to do this for one night. I'm not a creep. But ever since I've seen her, I can't help but want to be near her.

I've learned her schedule. At 9:15, she leaves her house to walk to the train. She gets on at 9:20 and rides for four stops total. When the train runs on time, she may stop for a chai tea—right, not coffee. If there are delays, she skips it altogether. She goes into the hospital building and stays until 6:30 PM. With that rigid schedule and formal attire, I guess she's an administrator of some sort. She often misses the 6:32 train and catches the next one before going straight home to order takeout.

She won't leave until the next morning. It's a quiet neighborhood where she lives—so uneventful that she doesn't even bother drawing the curtains, making it easy for me to see her. She spends the evening watching TV. She definitely enjoys sports and game shows. Sometimes she even yells at it.

I wonder which ones are her favorites. I want to know more, but how do I even approach her now? How can I ever look her in the eyes knowing I've invaded her privacy—and plan to keep doing it?

I keep saying that I'll stop, but deep down, I know that I won't. I've already signed up for all the meal delivery services just so I could be the one to deliver her nightly dinner order. I'm not sure which one she uses yet, so I've tried them all.

That's it! I can't keep doing this! At least tonight—enough is enough! I'm going home! My pants are damp from sitting on the ground anyway...

Oh my gosh! Was that a scream? It sounded like her! Is she in trouble?

I see her! She's looking this way! Wait! Can she see me?

And that's when she asked me the very question that had been haunting my thoughts: "What are you doing in the bushes?"

Number 84: I Left

Time Length: 120 seconds

Categories/Theme: Dramatic, Introspective, Relationships, Abuse, Empowerment, Emotional

Scene: A woman is telling her friend about her ex.

I know that I told him I wanted to still be friends. I truly believed I would miss him if I left for good. But I don't. I don't trust him anymore, so I don't miss him.

I don't miss his snide comments about everything I enjoyed. I can watch my favorite shows without hearing how stupid they are or how bad the actors are. I hated when he did that; it felt like he was calling me stupid too.

I love cooking more without him here. Nearly everything I made was considered "trash" to him. My food allergies seemed like an inconvenience for him—though I guess they kind of are for me too. Even more so, but I'm used to it.

Most of all, I don't miss the guilt he'd throw at me, especially when he wanted to be intimate and I would refuse. I wonder how long it's been since he last had sex? Who would even want to have sex with him now, anyway? I sure didn't... especially at the end.

I can't help but think about his mother. Does her husband treat her the same way her son treated me? Does she even know it's happening? I certainly didn't when it was happening to me. I wish I could help her, but I don't think I can. Would she have been happier had she not gotten pregnant? Had my ex and his brother never been born? Would she have escaped then? Were her sons the ones who convinced her to stay? Sons who don't even love her? When I think about it too much, it just makes me angrier.

I wonder if perhaps I loved this woman so much because we were always the same—two people pleasers wanting nothing more than to make the men we loved happy. Men who took advantage of us.

But we weren't the same. I wasn't born as her daughter; I'm my mother's daughter. My mother, who is strong, and I am strong like her. I was able to leave him because of that—nothing he could do, no amount of manipulation could change that.

I am my mother's daughter—a no-nonsense Jersey girl like her. And though I continuously beat myself up for not leaving that man sooner, it doesn't change the fact.

I left.

Number 85: Roommate Interrogation

Time Length: 120 seconds

Categories/ Theme: Dramatic, Law, Suspense, Investigation, Mysterious

Scene: A detective brings in the victim's roommate for questioning.

Hello, Mr. Sato. Thank you for coming in today. Do you know why we asked you to come here?

It's about your roommate. Yes, you said you were the one who discovered him. How did you exactly find him?

I see. So you share a room with him. And you woke up before the victim, correct? Where did you go that morning? To the gym. When you woke up, did you happen to notice if your roommate was breathing before you left? You claim he was snoring softly. What time did you return from the gym? 9 AM. And what did you do when you got back?

So you watched TV and had a snack in the living room. Then you got up to shower. Why didn't you shower at the gym? It was busy, you say. You claim other people might have seen you at the gym between 7 AM and 8:30 AM? Were any of these gym-goers friends of yours? Please write some of those names down for me, Mr. Sato.

Now, when you were on your way to shower, you stopped in your bedroom for a change of clothes. That's when you saw the victim still in bed? Did he look different from when you left? I see, you claim his arm was dangling lifelessly from the bed.

You ran over to check on him and he was dead. You say you first tried nudging him and took the pillow off his head. When you saw he wasn't breathing, that's when you dragged him onto the floor to perform CPR?

Mr. Sato, by any chance, did you leave the door open when you left for the gym that morning? You're not sure? Do you know anyone who might have wanted to hurt your roommate? And your relationship with the victim? You got along well as roommates? Never fought about chores? Perhaps a girl or two? No? You claim he was your best friend. Were you friends before becoming roommates? Since childhood, you say. And you don't know if the victim had any kind of fight prior to the incident? No one who might want to suffocate him with a pillow?

Okay, no more questions, Mr. Sato. We'll be in touch.

Number 86: I Hold a Candle

Time Length: 120 seconds

Categories/ Theme: Dramatic, Romance, Introspective, Metaphor, Love

Scene: The speaker discusses loving two people in a metaphoric way

When Levi and I first met, I lit a candle for him. A small one. I tucked it away in a corner of my heart, letting it burn quietly for him. It's still there, flickering, to this day.

Then came Jordan. For him, I lit the biggest candle I could find. I nurtured that flame and cared for it deeply. I loved Jordan very much, but I never completely forgot the candle I had lit for Levi. I'd find myself checking on it, reassured by its steady glow in that far corner—small, yet persistent beside the towering flame I'd lit for Jordan.

But as my relationship with Jordan grew unstable, storms began to rage in my heart. Gusts of wind grew stronger and stronger, threatening to extinguish both flames. Perched atop Jordan's candle, I felt the windstorm inhale for its next gust. Fear swept through me as I remembered how small Levi's candle was.

I leapt down from Jordan's candle and ran to the corner of my heart. "Levi!" I cried, shielding his flame with my body. The wind howled past, but Levi's candle survived.

When I looked up, I saw only a thin stream of smoke rising from Jordan's candle. Dread filled me as I scrambled back, crying, "No! No! But the candle was so big! The flame was so strong!"

By the time I reached the top, my greatest fear had come true. The flame was gone, and with it, my love for Jordan. I grieved for that extinguished light and the joy it once brought me. In the darkness, all I could feel was resentment for the man I once adored.

I hated this feeling. Desperately, I tried to relight Jordan's candle, succeeding only for short periods of time. I never got the flame back to what it once was. Soon, I knew I could no longer keep reviving it.

Even though I could still see the candle Jordan had lit for me burning brightly, I left him. What else could I do? The flame was gone.

(Pause)

I made my choice. In the end, I chose Levi.

Number 87: The Last Time I Saw Him

Time Length: 120 seconds

Categories/ Theme: Dramatic, Suspense, Relationships, Anxiety, Communication, Emotional

Scene: A person anxiously waiting for their partner to return from a potentially dangerous situation.

It's been four hours...

I've called his phone multiple times. I was supposed to pick him up at 6 AM, but he still hasn't called to tell me where he is.

(Dial the phone)

I really hope he's okay. Please be okay. Please don't be hurt or worse. Answer your phone!

I wonder if it got stolen. Could that be why he hasn't called yet? He doesn't have his phone anymore? He's had it off for three days while he's done that stupid social experiment with the homeless. The idiot didn't even want to take his phone, but I convinced him.

I hate that he does things like this. I thought dating a writer meant he was going to sit at home all day and cook meals for us. Which is the case most of the time, but sometimes he does research by immersing himself in unsafe situations—like pretending to be homeless in the most dangerous part of the city!

(Pause)

Stay calm… Stay calm… Just because he hasn't called does not mean he's dead…

But what if he is dead—or dying right now? What if someone hurt him?

I've gotta go look for him! I have to know if he's okay! These three days without him have been agonizing! He could have died right after I dropped him off. Oh my gosh, what if that was the last time I ever saw him?

(Pause)

Where should I look first? The streets? The hospital? No… If he was in the hospital, he would have called me to tell me he was there… So I guess that means…I have to go…to the m-morgue…

Oh my gosh.

(Call him again)

Pick up! Dammit! Pick up!

It just goes to voicemail… He's dead! My boyfriend is dead! And I might never actually find him!

I'm going to the police! I have to find him! I have to bring him home! I—

(Phone rings)

Oh my God! It's him!

(Answer it)

Where have you been? I've been worried sick! I was literally on my way to see if there was a thirty-something-year-old white dude at the morgue! Four hours, babe! You were asleep? Where are you? I'm coming to get you!

Number 88: Help Us from Our Godfather

Time Length: 120 seconds

Categories/ Theme: Dramatic, Suspense, Family, Conflict, Overcoming Adversity

Scene: A great aunt or uncle recants meeting children of a niece that needed help.

It looked like a normal sunny day when two little ones, a boy and a girl, showed up at my door, out of breath. The boy, clearly the older sibling, asked for me by name. When I confirmed, relief washed over their faces.

"Please help us," he said. "Our parents died recently, and we were sent to live with our godfather. We never met him before this, and our father never mentioned him. We thought he'd be stern and serious, like our dad.

"To our surprise, when our godfather arrived, he emerged from a fancy black sports car wearing a tailored suit and dark sunglasses. He approached me and asked, 'Are you the boy?'

"'Yes,' I replied. 'Are you our godfather?'

"'Yup. I'm the Godfather, alright. Now get in, you two.' So we did, and he took us to his mansion full of servants. I asked what he did for a living, and he said he ran a successful business. Then a worker came to him with news of a client arriving.

"Everything seemed fine—normal even—until I heard something that didn't seem right. It sounded like something being hit repeatedly, followed by screams of pain.

"I ran to my sister's room. 'Julie! I think our godfather is an actual godfather! We gotta get out of here now!'

"We left with only the bags we had brought. Once we were far enough away from the mansion, I dug around for my mother's phone that I had kept after she died. I unlocked it and searched her contacts for any distant relatives. We couldn't look at Dad's contacts because we didn't want our godfather to find us.

"Finally, we found your contact; it only had your address saved. We're so sorry to come here like this, but we're scared and miss our parents. Will you help us?"

I looked into the little boy's sad face and saw my beloved niece in his eyes; someone I had lost contact with years ago. I put my hands on their shoulders and led them inside.

"Come on in," I said. "We'll figure this out together."
The little boy began to cry and said, "I knew it! You did know our mom!"

Number 89: Worst Shopping Experience

Time Length: 120 seconds

Categories/ Theme: Humorous, Slice of Life, Situational, Shopping, Frustration

Scene: A woman shares with her friend a terrible experience shopping at the dollar store.

Let me tell you! I just had the absolute worst experience at the dollar store! I needed to buy some cookies, and since the weather was nice, I decided to take my e-scooter instead of my car. You know, saving gas and avoiding traffic. It put me in such a good mood that I ended up singing as I entered the store, scooter right beside me like always.

As I'm walking to the cookie aisle, I see a guy carrying a bag from my job's employee appreciation party, so I asked him if he was an employee. It's a big company with multiple warehouses, so it's not uncommon not to recognize everyone. He said he used to work there but recently quit.

Before our conversation continued, the cashier came over from her register and barked, "Excuse me! You need to put that up front!" She meant my scooter.

This wasn't my first time bringing it inside! I was offended by how she approached me. Sure, I look young, but her tone was unacceptable for one adult talking to another. So I responded firmly, "Absolutely not! I've never had an issue here before! I'm not leaving my scooter outside to get stolen!"

The cashier stormed off while the guy continued talking to me. Honestly, after standing up for myself, I wasn't really interested in chatting anymore, so I politely told him that I needed to grab what I came for and leave quickly. He agreed but then followed me into the next aisle to ask about my scooter—this thing is a man magnet!

He then asked me out on a date. Like I said, I just wanted to leave quickly, so I politely told him that I loved someone else—and he left me alone.

Later, when I checked out, that same cashier apologized and explained she wanted it up front—not outside—but I still refused that option. I depend on this scooter to get to work; losing it isn't an option for me! After paying for my snacks, I headed outside.

Just before hopping on my scooter to leave, a man loitering up front asked if I could spare anything. "No," I replied. "I just took my scooter to the dollar store to buy cookies!" Like seriously?

As I rode off, one thought crossed my mind: "The only thing that could have made this trip worse would be if the smoke alarm had gone off!"

Number 90: The Most Horrifying Place

Time Length: 120 seconds

Categories/ Theme: Humorous, Horror, Satire, Workplace, Mysterious, Imprisonment, Psychological

Scene: The speaker describes the most horrifying place that they can imagine.

Imagine a place where you're thrown into a box. A box just big enough for a desk and a chair. Inside that box, you perform the most monotonous tasks, one after another. The tasks keep coming—each more boring or confusing than the last. Each has a name, but they all sound the same.

You spend hours in that box, but don't think you have all day to complete each task. Each one has its own deadline, and it's up to you to manage them all. Forget one, and the consequences can be severe. These tasks may seem unimportant to you, but if you overlook one, it will wreak havoc on someone else.

That chair they give you? It's awful. As the hours drag on, your body sinks deeper into it. The cushioning disappears, leaving only hard edges poking at you. Standing offers brief relief, but these tasks won't complete themselves. So despite your aching bottom from sitting in the most uncomfortable chair imaginable, you sit.

And you continue to sit. You do this because you aren't completely alone in that box. Your every move is monitored. You have to report to the observer from time to time. He or she will determine your fate. Will you be given a bigger box? A more comfortable one? Or will you be ejected into the unknown?

There are other people in boxes all around you. You must decide whom to trust, but remember—never trust too much. Any one of them could be a snake. You'll be tempted to befriend them because you see them every day, but not all are safe. Any one of them could report you and have you cast out into the unknown.

You don't want to be sent there. You need this box to survive. Could you make it in the unknown if you knew more about it? Perhaps. But most cannot. Most people cannot survive outside the box.

What exactly is this box? Have you not figured it out yet? The box is an office—a cubicle in a corporate setting.

And that, my friend, is the most horrifying place of all.

Number 91: I'll Show You How It's Done, Little Boy

Time Length: 120 seconds

Categories/ Theme: Humorous, Animal/ Nature, Introspective, Mentorship, Family

Scene: A cat analyzes the younger cat that recently joined the family.

Ugh, there he goes again... That little imp! How does he have so much energy? It's only a matter of time until he jumps on me like he always does. I can't even play anymore because he takes that as an invitation. I wouldn't mind it if he weren't so rough. He's so much gentler when he plays with my humans. Why can't he do that with me?

I'll admit, he was fun when he was a kitten, but that didn't last long. Once he hit puberty, he became obsessed with me! I get it—I'm beautiful! My humans even tell me I'm the most beautiful cat they've ever had! But what makes him think I want anything to do with him? He's just a little boy to me! He's a baby...

At least he makes my humans happy. Truth be told, he's a great pet to them—sweet and playful. If only he weren't so damn annoying, I'd like him so much more. I'm getting older, though... When I die, my humans will be heartbroken. I hate that for them; I don't like it when they're sad. At least with him around, I know he'll take care of them when I'm gone. I love my humans, and I know he does too. He's a good boy.

Oh? Did our humans buy us a new toy? It's pretty big! Is this a tunnel? Awesome!

Huh? Oh... Looks like the little boy is afraid of it... Typical... That's definitely one of his major flaws—a scaredy cat! Oh, brother... There's no reason to be afraid of a new toy the humans bought you. Watch... I'll just sit in the middle of it and show you it's safe... Ridiculous little boy...

Yup! See? It's perfectly safe in here. You can come in...

Ah! The humans noticed what I'm doing! Yes, I'm showing this little dude how it's done. You're right, Mom and Sissy; I am a good girl!

Someone doesn't look scared anymore. And now he's running toward me... Time to go...

Hahaha! Now look at him—it's his favorite toy! Big sister Cookie to the rescue! Now everyone is happy. I'd say I did a job well done.

Number 92: A Best Friend

Time Length: 120 seconds

Categories/ Theme: Humorous, Relationships, Thematic, Friendship, Empowerment

Scene: A person describes what a best friend is to her.

A lot of people on the internet describe their best friend as the person who laughs at them when they fall. The person who teases them to the point where they are almost insulted. They describe the people who are kind and helpful to them as merely "just a friend."

That's not what I wanted in a best friend. I've been teased and bullied my whole life. The very last person who should kick me when I'm down is my bestie.

No, my bestie is the one who supports me! Who encourages my ideas no matter how big, dumb, crazy, or even somewhat evil they could be.

When someone does me wrong, my best friend doesn't criticize me or tell me how I must have screwed up. No, he recommends getting even. He says, "Let's go set their place on fire." We might even draft up a plan knowing full well that we are not going to go through with it. But we allow ourselves to journey down that solution and picture the satisfaction of burning up my enemy's property. We explore hurting them back solely for the feeling. And then he exclaims, "Burn it! Burn it to the ground!"

It makes us feel better. The situation no longer hurts me because in the worst-case scenario, we could set a fire. Usually, the problem isn't bad enough for us to do it. So we don't.

That's what a best friend means to me! Someone who believes I'm right even if I could be wrong. Someone who encourages me to pursue my dreams—the person who cheers me on as I chase after the unattainable career or celebrity.

When everyone else is laughing at me and telling me that I can't do it, my bestie shows me unwavering support. He believes I can and wants it for me just as much as I do. He will never tell me no; he's always in my corner. And worst-case scenario, he will come to my aid and hide the bodies.

But don't worry, we're good people, so it won't come to that. But don't think we don't have a plan in case it does.

By the way, my bestie agrees with me, and said, "If anyone has a problem with that, we'll burn them too!"

Number 93: Why Do They Keep Him?

Time Length: 120 seconds

Categories/ Theme: Humorous, Workplace, Frustration, Overhearing

Scene: Two coworkers discuss another coworker in the office.

I don't know how that old guy gets away with it. One second, he's having personal calls one after another; the next, he's falling asleep at his desk with his mouse still in hand.

I mean, I get that sometimes you need to take a personal call or two at your desk, but every day? Do you think he ever gets any work done? And his conversations often have sensitive information in them! Do you know his address? I do! 213 Elmwood Lane! I swear, if I'm ever lost without my phone in the city, I might just go there!

He has these full-on conversations at his desk! He almost never goes into the other room! He could be having a full argument with his wife right there! He'll be all, "Tova, can I talk? Can I speak now?" I think Tova is his wife, but every time he makes a doctor's appointment for her, he calls her Naomi! I don't get it!

I could never ask him about his conversations either... Oh, you know I can't! That grumpy old man would bite my head off! I can't say two words to him without him trying to get under my skin! I think it's deliberate!

You do much better with him than I do! I've heard how he talks to you! He can be such a jerk—so defensive at times. Like when you were working on that document together and had the boss look it over before he was ready to submit? Why did he get so angry at you? It's not like the boss expected it to be perfect; he just wanted to see the progress, right? Yeah! And he got so angry at you. It was so unprofessional!

What? You said the boss wants me to teach him a program? Oh! Hell no! I can't teach him anything! I can't even talk to him! No! Absolutely not! If the boss asks, my answer is no! I have the right to work in a productive environment, and working with him would make it hostile!

While I sometimes find his personal conversations interesting and even funny, the best thing for me is to stay as far away from that old goat as possible! I don't know how you can stand it! Why doesn't he just retire already? It's time! Why do they keep him around?

Number 94: My First Roller Coaster Ride

Time Length: 120 seconds

Categories/ Theme: Wistful, Thematic, Childhood, Adventure

Scene: An adult reminisces about their first experience on a roller coaster

I love roller coasters! I'll never forget my first one.

I was nine, and my aunt took me and three of her kids to the local amusement park. My cousins kept checking in on me, asking if I was ready. I assured them I was. When they suggested trying a coaster with loops, I decided to be brave and said yes.

We waved goodbye to my aunt and youngest cousin, who was too small to ride, and got in line for the coaster named after a Greek monster. I counted the loops as we waited for our turn. Was it seven or six? It was hard to tell from where we were standing. Honestly, it made no difference. My cousins said this ride was fun, so I trusted them.

Finally, it was our turn. We boarded the car, and I sat between my cousins—my braver cousin on the end. Once the ride was secured and the two employees—who I remember as being muscular men—gave the thumbs up, the girl at the station hit the button, and the floor folded away below us.

The car pulled forward. I listened to the clicking of the conveyor with anticipation as we reached our highest point. My cousin on the end pointed and said, "Look! You can see the animals in the other park!"

"Oh! Cool!" I said. Then with one last click, the coaster car stopped moving for just a second before it descended.

The wind rushed quickly in my face—faster than I'd ever felt before! My eyes weren't used to that sensation; they began watering as if I were crying. I started screaming—I mean, I was on a very fast roller coaster after all! My cousin turned to ask if I was okay, and I was fine—my eyes were watering terribly, but honestly? I was having a great time!

And then the ride halted to a sudden stop. We were released from our harnesses and returned to my aunt.

She asked, "Did you have fun?"

I felt a little unsteady on my feet but replied, "Yeah! That was awesome!"

Then she handed me a card and said, "Here's a present for you." Inside was a picture of us on the ride. I could tell it was taken right when my cousin checked in on me because her head was turned away from the camera. Man, did I look miserable! It's hilarious because later that day, I rode almost all the rides and got season passes for the next year.

I still have that picture. I'll never forget that day!

Number 95: Cookie

Time Length: 120 seconds

Categories/ Theme: Wistful, Animal/ Nature, Grief, Emotional, Thematic

Scene: A cat owner describes a beloved pet.

She was the last pet of my childhood, and I'll never forget how gentle and kind Cookie was. I would sit there, staring into her almond eyes with that white eyeliner, cooing, "I love you," over and over again. She'd respond with slow blinks in rhythm with my voice, looking like she was smiling—a cat's smile that all cat owners recognize. Her purr wasn't loud; sometimes you had to get close to hear it, but she made up for it with her affection.

Cookie was one of my most playful cats. She didn't play with my hands—far too gentle for that—but she loved games. When she was young, she would play fetch with toys or even a plastic straw. But her favorite game was tag! In our cape cod home, I'd pretend to hide, and if she wanted to play, she'd stalk me before charging at me! I'd scream then laugh and then I chased her back. It was tag after all so we took turns on who was "it."

When my new kitten arrived, he used to drive her nuts. He just wanted to play but was just too rough. She stopped playing tag because he would pounce on her, changing the game entirely. I felt bad that we adopted him when she clearly didn't want a little brother, but we just couldn't turn away a kitten on Christmas.

In her final days, Cookie seemed at peace with him around. We had one last good Christmas together—she played with boxes and touched noses with him for a picture. It was her last really good day before she slowly declined.

The night before she was put to sleep, I said goodnight like always. She gave me that look of love but moaned when trying to sit up. I petted her and thanked her for telling me she was in pain. I knew it was our last night together, so I said my mantra one last time, "Good night, kitten. I love you more than all the other kittens."

Losing Cookie was one of the hardest losses of my life. With family members, you can pretend they're still alive because you don't see them daily. But with a pet, there's no escape from it—the creature you cared for in your home is gone, and it's a grief you just have to face.

Number 96: Featured from All Because of an Apple

Time Length: 120 seconds

Categories/ Theme: Introspective, Self-Discovery, Dramatic, Bullying, Conflict, Slice of Life

Scene: The main character has an odd obsession with living each day exactly the same every day. He finally opens up to someone as to why.

Since I was being harassed at school by Michael and at home by my parents, I decided to follow the oldest advice for bullying: don't react. I implemented a rigid schedule at home that worked well with dealing with my parents, so I decided to take it a step further and follow an even stricter schedule at school.

I left home at exactly 6:47 am and arrived at school at exactly 7:15 am. I left all my classes at the same time, even if the teacher insisted that they did not dismiss me. I went to my locker at the same time too, making sure to go when Michael wouldn't be there.

To not attract unnecessary attention among my classmates, I no longer participated in class. Teachers would call on me, but I refused to answer. I got sent to the office multiple times about that; I just didn't go. My grades didn't suffer so eventually the teachers gave up.

I had a schedule to keep. It helped me stay motivated throughout the day. Eventually, my perseverance paid off. Michael no longer bothered me. In fact, no one bothered with me at school ever again. I talked so little at the lunch table that my acquaintances wanted nothing to do with me, so I ate alone.

I successfully became invisible. And despite having to follow such a strict schedule, I felt liberated. I no longer had to deal with social conflict again.

My schedule became a safe space for me, but also pretty boring. When I thought about loosening up on my schedule even a little bit though, I couldn't help but remember my life before implementing it. So instead of relaxing it, I made it even stricter.

So here I am. I became so comfortable with following my perfectly crafted schedule that I no longer remember who I was before, so I just stayed the same.

Number 97: She Owes Me

Time Length: 120 seconds

Categories/ Theme: Introspective, Dramatic, Relationships, Psychological, Manipulation

Scene: An ex boyfriend waits at the stage door for his ex.

There she is! It's really her. I can't believe it. We were together for five years, and I rarely heard her sing. I had no idea she would turn it into a career. She used to beg me to take her to the theater, and now look at her—on stage every day with those people she found so interesting.

I still don't get it. What's so great about them? Why did she try so hard to become one of them? Does she even have any identity of her own? She just follows whatever tiny interest she has and throws herself into it full force.

Why does she even do it? Does she need that much recognition from others? That's so sad. If she had stayed with me, I could have taught her how to be happy. She'll never know what it means to be truly happy because she's out there trying to be a star with all these wannabes instead of living a life more suitable for her.

I knew what was best for her. I proved it every single time. She can't do anything for herself; she has no sense of self, which is why she's here on stage.

She looks happy, but I know that's a lie. She was happy with me. She loved me. She'll never forget me. I'm the one who made her dreams come true and offered her safety and financial support. Everything she has is because of me.

Here she comes. Now I will remind her what her duty is. She will look into my eyes and see that she made a mistake six years ago when she left me. She should have stayed home and catered to my needs. She owes that to me.

(To the ex)

Hi, Kitten! You were amazing up there! Oh, you remember me! I thought you would have forgotten all about me, Kitten. You're doing so well! Let me know if you want to catch up sometime—I'm doing really well too! I've made huge improvements to my house and—

Oh, you gotta go? Okay... Well, bye, Kitten! Can I call you later? No? Are you busy? Yeah, I guess you just did this huge performance and everything. Okay, Kitten, it's good to see you! Have a good show tomorrow!

Number 98: Pappy's Blanket

Time Length: 120 seconds

Categories/ Theme: Wistful, Family, Life Lesson, War Story

Scene: A grandchild describes a family story.

I have a war story about my grandfather! No, he never spoke of taking out any Nazis, but he was able to use his own skills to help out as a cook. Feeding an army is a very important job to do, so I'm proud of him and his contribution!

I like this story about him though. Apparently, they gave each soldier a bag of personal supplies that he would be responsible for. Likely it included rations, weapons, ammo, change of socks and etc., but the last item that was given was a blanket.
The troops started their tour of the European warzone in Italy. As the war continued, the troops had to move around. The longer they stayed in certain areas, the warmer it got. Soon soldiers started throwing away their blankets to have less to carry around with them.

As more time passed and more humid days dragged on, nearly all blankets were abandoned, except for one. My grandfather, despite being the cook and having to carry around cooking materials along with his war supplies, held onto his blanket.
Other soldiers tried to convince him to throw it away, but he declined. He would say, "No, that's okay. I don't mind carrying it," or, "Ah, it's not that heavy," or, "I love having a blanket. You never know when you might need it."

And need it, he did. After months of trekking around, the troops were eventually sent to colder regions and winter loomed closer.

On a blustery night, all the soldiers huddled together around the fire, struggling to keep warm. They eventually had to turn into their tents to sleep uncomfortably in the chilly evening air. All but one had an awful night: my grandfather. After months of lugging around the wool blanket in the heat, he was rewarded with the comfort of a warm goodnight's sleep.

From that moment on, I used my grandfather as an example of how hard work pays off. Sometimes it's a struggle, but sometimes struggling is the smartest thing to do in the long run.

My grandfather later opened his own restaurant after the war, teaching me that we should all focus on our natural abilities to build a better life for ourselves.

Number 99: Happy Birthday to my Dear Uncle

Time Length: 120 seconds

Categories/ Theme: Wistful, Dramatic, Family, Grief, Conflict, Emotional

Scene: A niece or nephew processes grief of an uncle on his birthday.

It's your birthday today. Happy birthday. I wish you were here to celebrate with us.

I've changed since you left. I'm still pursuing my art business, expanding into different mediums.

You know, I'm still mad at you. It's true that I miss you, but we never got to discuss our issues before you died. I wanted to bring it up, but I wasn't sure if you were in the right state of mind to listen. I know you were sick, and the last thing you needed was for me to complain about my problems.

You were my role model in business! You worked remotely before it was a thing, had this big house, your wife didn't work, and all your children had their own rooms. I wanted to be like you.

To my surprise, you didn't support my business at all! From day one, you told me it was going to fail. You treated my artwork like a hobby instead of the craft I'd dedicated my whole life to. You made me feel like a loser, a mooch off my parents, and an absolute idiot!

Well, guess what! My business is failing now. I hope you're happy! Yes, I said I was expanding it, but all the confidence in any of my ideas working is long gone. I'm going to fail, just like you said I would, yet I keep trying anyway because I can't stop! I don't want to...

Why couldn't you just help me? If my business plan was so awful, why didn't you give me advice on how to improve it? You had all the experience!

Look! Now you're dead! And you never apologized! Now this is gonna cloud my memories of you forever...

I'm sorry for wanting so much from you. You were only trying to help the only way you knew how. Whether or not I ever deserved an apology, I miss you. Happy birthday.

Number 100: A Man Dies on a Deserted Island

Time Length: 120 seconds

Categories/ Theme: Wistful, Dramatic, Philosophical, Isolation, Emotional, Grief

Scene: A man died in his sleep. There is only one person on the deserted island to witness his passing. That person is contemplating his or her feelings on the loss of life.

I think it's been at least an hour since his last breath. There was nothing I could do. It's dark outside now and I'm just too drained to move him. I can't bring myself to roll him onto the cold ground. He still feels so warm…

One more night with him. Just one. I know he's nothing but a corpse now, but he was a person only moments ago. Someone with purpose, potential. Now, everything is gone…

I wonder if he had a family wherever he came from. I wonder if they have any idea where he is. Does he have a mother, a father? Do they somehow know in their hearts that their beloved son is dead? Does he have any friends that'll miss him? Cousins? Siblings? Children? A girlfriend or wife? Will any of them know that on an island in the middle of nowhere, far out to somewhere this nameless man that they have a name for breathed his last?

No… I suppose they don't.

Perhaps they can go on believing that he's still just missing. Perhaps, they have hope that they'll find him again someday.

The only one who knows the truth of his demise is a young twenty-three year old who will never return home again.

With this man's last breath, I not only lost a potential partner on this island, I lost all the potential answers he could have given me. Where did he come from? Why was he here? Just who was this once very handsome man?

How could I grieve so? Ignorance was supposed to be bliss, but how could I be blissful when all my hope and all my new dreams died right before my eyes? What could he have taught me? How could we have survived together? Could we have figured out a way off the island together? Could we have lived here together forever in paradise?

I'll never know. I can't know!

Number 101: Doing This for Love

Time Length: 120 seconds

Categories/ Theme: Introspective, Dramatic, Inspirational, Self-Discovery, Love

Scene: An aspiring performer questions and scrutinizes her own motives.

I keep asking myself, why am I doing this? And my heart answers firmly, without hesitation: for love. But who is it that I love? Where is this love being directed? Am I doing this for the love of him? Are all the classes, the shows, the long hours practicing, the networking, is this all for him? Do I truly love him that much?

Surely that's true. In fact, I know it! I love him enough to turn my world upside down and become the person who I've always dreamed to be. To leave the current unsatisfying life that I have and follow after him. To dance for him despite how much it hurts. Like the little mermaid from Hans's original tale.

But women are told not to act like the little mermaid. It's frowned upon to change your whole life just for a man. Which brings me back to my original question: Why am I doing this? Do I truly love him enough to work this hard? To put myself out there and break my comfort zone? To risk a regular, secure life for one of uncertainty?

I listen to my heart once more and I know the answer with certainty... All of this is not just for him. He is merely a driving factor. He is a best-case scenario, a guide, a dream to something bigger! A leader to my true self, a light in the pathway so I know which direction to go! I wanted to be a performer my whole life! How could I have forgotten? I didn't forget; I just didn't believe that I could! That's why I will stop listening to the negative thoughts and the equally negative people around me. I follow him to my destiny. My muse, my angel, my inspiration to be... truly me.

So I have my answer! This is all for love! Love for him, love for my crafts—all of them—and most of all, love for myself that I haven't shown before! That is the love that drives me! That is why I do this!

About the Author

Picture taken by Laura Knewasser

    Daughter of a Photographer and a Facility Manager, Jessica Knewasser was born in Princeton, New Jersey and lived in Burlington County her whole life. It was from her mother that she learned the value of art and following her dreams while her father taught her about the value of hard work. She studied Business and Management at Mercer County Community College and The College of New Jersey.
    After publishing her first manga, *Over My Dead Body, Volume 1* in 2019, she decided to take voice lessons with Aaron Cafaro in Hamilton, NJ, and found that not only did she enjoy singing, but she was really good. She decided to start auditioning around Central Jersey and got her first role as the Town Miller at the New Jersey Renaissance Faire. Then she auditioned for Thank You 5's production of "School of Rock," at

Kelsey Theatre and got picked to be in the adult ensemble playing: a groupie, Summer's Mom, a teacher and a waitress. These experiences inspired her to start writing monologues and she further studied acting with Renee Weisband in Moorestown, NJ.

When she created her company, Knewasser Productions, she never stated that it was solely a manga company. Rather, it's a literary company, so despite the flagship product being her manga series, *101 Relatable Monologues* is the first of what she hopes are many more literary projects outside of manga. She believes that there are principles of fiction writing and only the true writer knows what is best for his or her characters. Whether it's manga, monologues or any other literary project in the future, she promises that every story she creates is original and created for the characters by the characters. She hopes that in turn, you, as the reader, will reap the benefits of her works.

To see more of her work, (including singing and performance updates) you can follow her on Facebook, Instagram, Tapas via: https://tapas.io/knewasserproductions or at www.kpmanga.com.

Index

Abuse: 75, 77, 81, 166, 172

Adventure: 14, 17, 193

Afterlife: 21, 31, 44, 47, 57

Ambition: 83, 105, 147

Animal/Nature: 91, 97, 145, 149, 187, 195

Anxiety: 27, 67, 105, 115, 121, 137, 178

Art: 95, 137, 153

Authority: 19, 33

Breaking Point: 65, 107

Bullying: 16, 197

Childhood: 52, 111, 113, 193

Communication: 23, 28, 30, 35, 52, 95, 178

Conflict: 19, 21, 27, 28, 32, 37, 57, 69, 81, 83, 85, 91, 93, 117, 160, 166, 170, 181, 197, 203

Cultural: 40, 99, 139, 155

Customer Service: 23, 28, 109

Daydreaming: 51

Descriptive: 139, 145

Dramatic: 14, 16, 17, 19, 45, 47, 49, 54, 57, 59, 61, 63, 65, 67, 69, 71, 73, 75, 77, 79, 81, 83, 85, 115, 117, 119, 125, 127, 137, 141, 143, 147, 153, 160, 162, 164, 166, 168, 170, 172, 174, 176, 178, 181, 197, 199, 203, 205, 207

Emotional: 61, 67, 85, 115, 143, 157, 168, 172, 195, 203, 205

Empowerment: 75, 79, 129, 131, 133, 135, 172, 189

Ethics: 47, 71, 73, 123, 170

Exorcism: 44

Family: 29, 52, 59, 99, 111, 115, 181, 187, 201, 203

Fantasy: 14, 49, 57, 59, 141, 153

Food: 28, 38, 42

Friendship: 16, 25, 69, 95, 162, 189

Frustration: 21, 31, 32, 37, 85, 87, 107, 119, 125, 129, 166, 183, 191

Grief: 195, 203, 205

Health: 30, 71, 125, 143

Historical Fiction: 61, 93, 153, 155

Horror: 44, 63, 113, 185

Humorous: 21, 23, 25, 27, 28, 29, 30, 31, 32, 33, 35, 37, 38, 40, 42, 44, 51, 69, 87, 89, 91, 93, 95, 97, 99, 101, 103, 105, 107, 109, 111, 113, 115, 117, 133, 149, 183, 185, 187, 189, 191

Imprisonment: 61, 65, 185

Informative: 99, 123, 133

Innovation: 93

Inspirational: 131, 135, 147, 207

Introspective: 42, 49, 59, 77, 79, 83, 97, 119, 121, 123, 125, 127, 129, 131, 133, 135, 137, 157, 160, 172, 176, 187, 197, 199, 207

Investigation: 33, 174

Isolation: 17, 205

Justice System: 103, 127, 151

Law: 33, 103, 127, 151, 174

Life Lesson: 201

Love: 51, 54, 141, 155, 157, 160, 162, 176, 207

Manipulation: 81, 117, 164, 166, 199

Medical: 71, 125, 143

Mentorship: 151, 187

Metaphor: 176

Misunderstanding: 14, 19, 25, 37, 40, 45, 89, 111, 141

Morality: 27, 123, 127, 170

Mysterious: 174, 185

Overcoming Adversity: 17, 75, 77, 145, 168, 181

Overhearing: 35, 101, 191

Philosophical: 205

Political: 123

Psychological: 14, 65, 121, 170, 185, 199

Relationships: 27, 29, 30, 35, 45, 51, 75, 77, 79, 81, 83, 85, 87, 91, 101, 115, 135, 149, 162, 166, 172, 178, 189, 199

Renaissance Faire: 93, 155

Revenge: 57, 164

Romance: 21, 31, 49, 51, 54, 73, 141, 155, 157, 176

Satire: 89, 103, 113, 185

Sci-fi: 73, 89, 162

Self-Discovery: 16, 45, 49, 54, 59, 67, 77, 131, 137, 139, 147, 151, 197, 207

Shopping: 38, 42, 183

Situational: 32, 69, 87, 89, 91, 93, 95, 103, 105, 109, 168, 183

Slice of Life: 16, 25, 27, 28, 29, 30, 32, 33, 35, 38, 42, 97, 101, 107, 109, 145, 149, 183, 197

Social Commentary: 47, 79, 119, 123, 129, 133, 135

Supernatural: 21, 25, 31, 44, 57, 63, 113, 164

Suspense: 17, 65, 164, 168, 170, 174, 178, 181

Technology: 23, 47, 73, 87

Thematic: 29, 111, 113, 121, 129, 131, 160, 168, 189, 193, 195

Thoughtful: 45, 47, 52, 99, 121

Tragedy: 63

Transformation: 63, 162

Travel: 40, 139

War Story: 201

Wistful: 51, 52, 54, 139, 141, 143, 145, 147, 149, 151, 153, 155, 157, 193, 195, 201, 203, 205, 207

Workplace: 19, 23, 37, 67, 101, 105, 107, 109, 117, 119, 185, 191

In Loving Memory of Jerry Mamola

September 29, 1961 — April 9, 2023

I will never forget your fun and goofy nature,
Uncle JerrymaBob

Love,
Niece Jessimaca

www.ingramcontent.com/pod-product-compliance
Lightning Source LLC
Chambersburg PA
CBHW072155070526
44585CB00015B/1147